Here's what others are saying about "Walking Down Life's Path"

"Written with a reminiscent voice full of fondness that almost makes those who are too young to have experienced "The 60s and 70s" yearn for its simplicity." -*Laeia Jackson-Author of "Crimson Ink"*

"I previewed your book and it really made me smile. I love how you described the 60's & 70's. It really brought back some great memories. And the embarrassing stories, just made me laugh. A book like this could really brighten someone's day." -*Laura Vargas -Author of "100 Reasons Not to Kill Yourself"*

I've read this book cover-to-cover and I really loved it. It was interesting, informative and hilariously funny. Barb has a great sense of humor. The thing I like most about Barb's memoirs is that in spite of having many hard knocks from life, she's always come out on the other side saying, "Well, I learned this from that experience and now I'm ready to move on." This book is terrific. -*Leslie Jones, Writing critique group*

Walking Down Life's Path

(Memoirs)

Author: Barbara A. Foley
Photographer: Barbara A. Foley

Walking Down Life's Path (Memoirs)

Printed by Lulu Enterprises, Inc.

Published by Barbara A. Foley

For more information:
http://www.lulu.com

Barbara A. Foley, Pennsylvania

Photo on Front Cover: Tallyrand Park, Bellefonte, PA

First Edition

Online at http://stores.lulu.com/bfoley

Library of Congress Control Number: 2008934094

ISBN 978-0-6152-2383-4

Barb (age 3) Raystown, Huntingdon, PA

Landon and Pap (John) Photo taken in 2008

Acknowledgments

I want to thank John, my husband, and Landon, my grandson, who was patient with me while doing this book.

Pennsylvania State Flower
Mountain Laurel

Contents

Contents

How To Read This Book:

You can read this book cover to cover, or read a story that interests you first. These stories are not in any particular order, and are bits and pieces of the first half of my life between, 1960 to 2008. I hope to have a lot more stories in years to come.

All information in this book is true, only a few names have been changed to conceal their identities. In that case, I have indicated that in *italic* at the beginning of the story.

Thanks for picking up this book.

•

Santa Taking A Train Ride

Note: (Here's a letter Landon received from Santa. I wanted to include it for him.)

Christmas 2007

Dear Landon,

It's been cold and snowing here at the North Pole. The Elves and I are getting ready for our long trip to visit you and all the good boys and girls. I've heard you been especially good this year. That's wonderful! I'm so glad because I didn't want to miss your house.

Rudolph told me to tell you he says; "hello," and can't wait to stop by your house. You might hear hooves on the roof late on Christmas Eve, but not to worry. That will be my reindeer and me.

Have you made your Christmas list this year yet? I've heard that you want a four-wheeler, Sponge Bob Square Pants, and some action figure guys. I'm sure you will let me know if there is anything else special that you want this year. If you'd like to stop by to see me, it would be wonderful to see you in person. If not, I will be around on Christmas Eve. Not to worry if I haven't covered that special gift, my Elves will let me know. We hear everything.

Did you know that when my Elves aren't working they are outside having snowball fights? Those Elves! Although, I must tell you, one hit me right in the back of the head. I am fine though.

Well, I must go. I have more letters to write and little time. Mrs. Claus is telling me it's time to eat. I must be able to fit into my suit by Christmas. Please leave out the milk and cookies if you want, they are my favorite.

See you Christmas Eve,

Love,

Santa Claus

End Note: (Landon did a lot of whispering after he got his letter from Santa. He says, "Santa hears everything.")

A First Grade Christmas

Do you remember black and white TVs, flower power, the love bug car, record players, bell-bottoms, lava lamps, 8-track tape players, disco and President Kennedy? I grew up in the 60s and 70s and started school in the first grade. Kindergarten wasn't mandatory then and show and tell was the "in" thing at school. The class was told to bring something we'd gotten at Christmas to show and tell after the Christmas break.

That year at home, like many other Christmases, we didn't get a lot of toys because our family was struggling to put food on the table. When I woke up Christmas morning, waiting for me under the tree was a baby doll, a few doll outfits, a coloring book and crayons, clothes and a Sears catalog. My sister and I had received the Sears catalog as a present because we had wanted to cut it up to play paper dolls. My mom would never let us destroy the catalog until she had picked some things out of it to tell Santa to bring. We then would get the catalog as a present and after it was wrapped, then opened, that was our indication we were allowed to cut it up.

Since my Christmas gifts were slim, I decided not to take my prize doll for show and tell. I had thought about it long and hard. The cons of taking my doll outweighed the pros. I had decided on the coloring book and crayons.

Everyone at school wanted their prized Christmas gifts to be a secret until time to talk about it in front of the class. Most of the other kids felt they had the best toy ever. The boys brought their cars, trucks and GI Joes. A few girls had a fancy dress but most of them had their bigger dolls, tea sets and Barbie dolls. Then it was my turn. I knew after seeing their Christmas gifts, I was in trouble. I should have brought the doll.

I stood up with hesitation and the teacher told me to show the class what I had brought. I slowly held up my coloring book and crayons and the whole class started laughing and teasing me. I wanted to run and hide.

5

"Stop laughing" the teacher pleaded to the class, and then proceeded to try and make me feel better. Embarrassed and hurt, I knew I did have something better than those crayons and that coloring book. It was my doll! When I tried to tell the class that I had a doll at home they didn't believe me. I was only six years old and felt even smaller. The teasing went on for a few days and then the other children went on to something or someone else.

Collectibles

Have you ever thought about why and when you started collecting something? How did you decide to collect what you do? Do you even have a collection? If not, why? Some people like to save a collection that they may have inherited, even if they don't like it. I personally have to really love what I want to collect.

Janet, my sister, purposely went out to find something to collect. I started a collection and she wanted to do the same. So, one day we set out to the stores to find something she was interested in collecting. Finally she settled on Indian items because Pocahontas always fascinated her. I never understood why she didn't choose horses, as she always loved horses even as a child.

My brother-in-law, Denny, collects old records. I'm not so sure it was intended to be a collection, except for the fact records are no longer available and he can't part with them. Now they are collectables.

John, my husband, collects golf balls because he loves to play golf. He thought it would be a great idea to collect golf balls with the names of places where we travel. John also collects State Police model cars and patches. He doesn't collect local police, just state police. Being a State Trooper this is a collection he can relate to. John at one point was going to collect snakes, mainly cobras, but I asked him; "where are you ever going to find cobras?" Now, we see them everywhere, but he has lost the interest to collect them, even though he really likes them.

Lucas, my oldest son, collects canes and walking sticks. He has always liked whittling wood and loves the carvings on them. He probably started around the age of eighteen. Mitch, my younger son, has been collecting swords since he was around fourteen years old. He has always handled them responsibly. Mitch also has been interested in Ninja collections.

Landon, my grandson, age five, has been collecting PEZ dispensers for the past year. He loves them and wanted to display them. He now owns a little over one hundred. We have slacked off buying them as much now so we can see if it's something he will still want when he gets older. He loves looking at them.

My mom used to collect lots of figurines. I can remember as a teenager having to dust them off every week and she had a whole case full. She decided they were just dust collectors after a while and has since gotten rid of them all and now only has a few items displayed in her house. It's kind of funny, as much as she loves hummingbirds she has never collected them. My dad also has a love for hummingbirds, so I'm surprised they don't collect them. They do love to sit on the porch and watch the real ones. My dad is what you call a collector of everything. When he goes to auctions and sees something he thinks is a good deal, he will bid on it. My mom then just tells him to get rid of the junk. You could say he is a collector of tools since he has just about all of them, but he doesn't think of them as a collection.

Then there are my own collections. I first started collecting carousel horses in 1993. I remember that year because it is the year we got married. John bought me my first carousel horse while we were in Arizona on our honeymoon. I had always loved carousel horses even as a child. I love the music as well as all the details on them. I probably now own a little over thirty carousels, from horses to merry-go-rounds, to other animals that I can find that would be on a carousel ride. I also have carousel tokens, plates and postage stamps. Carousel horses are harder to find now because most of the places that made them went out of business.

I also have a skunk collection, mostly Pepe LePew, along with teapots and plates with skunks painted on them. I have decided to get rid of most of my skunk collection. My kitchen is done in skunk collectables with hangings of skunk lithographs on the wall. I still love skunks and had owned a real one for about seven years, but I feel it is time to redo the

8

kitchen in a more grown-up look. I will, however, probably not part with my skunk plates and teapots. I still never get tired of looking at those.

My last collection is my folk art teapots. I only have four, but I love folk art teapots and folk art paintings. I will probably get rid of one of my teapots as that one doesn't interest me much and it's not really folk art. I have a "Hickory, Dickory, Dock" teapot and I have grown tired of it.

These aren't the only things I wanted to collect. I also love butterflies. At one time I was going to collect them, but decided we just didn't have the space for them. I'm glad I hadn't started that collection because I am trying to downsize my collections. I really like Ukrainian eggs, but only collect the ones that I hand made myself. That is something I am practicing doing and am trying to improve.

I believe if you do have a collection, you should at least have a passion for it. I don't see the point of collecting anything someone talks you into or keeping a collection you inherited if you are not interested in it. It seems collections have a way of growing if you don't put the brakes on. You could end up with a huge house full. But, just because you love something doesn't mean you have to collect it either. I will always love skunks and enjoy having them as pets, but it is sometimes best to move on and just get rid of the stuff.

When is it time to get rid of a collection? When you find it is no longer fun to collect or it has become more of a chore to keep up with it. I guess that's why my mom had gotten rid of her collectibles. She found it a chore to keep up with the dusting. And, when you start calling it stuff instead of a collection, then you know maybe it's time to part with it. I still call my carousels collectibles. I am now calling my skunk collection…stuff.

Anger

What do you do when you get angry? There are many ways to vent your anger. Myself, I vent in different ways depending on where I am. Sometimes, I hold it in too long to the point where I want to explode. Other times I try and talk to the person right away. If it's a boss or someone you need to be cautious of, I will try to work it out in my head before talking to them.

One day about twelve years ago or so, I was making chili for dinner. My two teen boys were being rowdy and fighting about something. I just don't remember what the bickering was about anymore. I was in the kitchen chopping onions and cooking hamburger to add with the beans and tomato sauce. After yelling at them several times to quit fighting, I started chopping hot peppers …and more hot peppers … and even more hot peppers. The chopping knife came down on each piece like someone hammering on a nail as fast as they could. I added them all. We then sat down to eat. I told the family not to say a word and they'd better eat the chili I put in their bowls. Everyone's face started getting fiery red. Not a word was spoken they just ate their food. Sweat started pouring from everyone's faces, including mine. We all got up for some water. Later on that night, the bathroom seemed to be in full use. I have never made chili since then that hot, but my family reminds me now and again about what they call my "firehouse chili". We can laugh about it now.

Then one time when my oldest son, Luke, was around eleven years old, I received a call at work saying to come and get my son that he had stolen a candy bar from a local grocery store. I was so mad when I got home, I couldn't speak to him. I grabbed the dog and started to walk, trying to cool down before talking to him. That poor little dog had never walked so fast in his life. I think he had to run to catch up to my walk. Now I know what speed walking is. When I got home I was cooled

10

down enough to have a conversation with Luke. I explained it wasn't right and we'd have to go and make it right with the storeowner. When Saturday came we went to see the manager. I asked him what he thought would be an appropriate punishment and he said; "how about two Saturdays working here?" I said; "that's not enough". "We'll take four Saturdays." I offered to pay for the candy bar Luke had taken, but the manager said that Luke working it off would be enough. He had told me most parents when they find out their child has stolen something just come in yelling at him, that their child would never do such a thing. They had told me they had seen my son taking it through their two-way mirror. I had no reason not to believe him. Luke did his four weeks of work and learned a valuable lesson.

There are also other ways to vent. Sometimes I will do some scrapbooking. It seems to have a calming effect. Other times just taking a walk will do the trick. Lately, as I have gotten older, I will start to clean when I get really mad. My husband usually knows when something is bugging me if all the dishes are done, and clutter has been cleared off the table, or the floors mopped when they aren't needed to be. A bad thing to do when I'm mad is to eat. I do get ice cream or chips out sometimes when I'm mad and that's the worse. When you eat your anger it only leads to two problems. The original problem you had to deal with, and now the weight you need to take off.

Luckily, I don't get so mad or angry over little things anymore. Actually, I don't think most of the things I was angry at were little. They were mostly big things, at least to me. I do however like to calm down if I am really angry before talking to the person that has made me that mad. I will stew on something until I can't take it any longer and then try to work out what I want to say before I pay them a visit. I will tell them what's on my mind and then it will be over and done with. Sometimes it helps, sometimes it doesn't, but it's always better to get it off your chest.

Famous People
I've Met and Wish I've Met

It was a wet and rainy day at the Clearfield Fair in the early 70s. Going to the fair was exciting for us because this was rare as money was always tight. My sister and I had just finished riding some rides and playing a few games. I had won a purple and white teddy bear that I was very proud of and after winning this medium sized bear, I was on cloud nine. We headed to the grandstand with my parents. I was to meet my first movie star. Roy Clark was famous for his singing and comedy on the TV show Hee-Haw. Roy was an expert at playing the banjo and other musical instruments.

The first one to come out on stage was Festus from the TV show "Gunsmoke". This was a bonus because I don't think my parents knew he was going to be there. My dad enjoyed watching this show and Festus looked exactly like he did on TV. He had his cowboy boots on with the spurs that clanged when he walked, a scarf around his neck and a dirty looking beard.

When Roy Clark came on stage, I felt my foot slipping. The ground was slippery from all the rain, and all I could think about was my prize bear. As I was falling, I thought, "save the bear at all costs!" Save him I did. I held him straight up in the air so he wouldn't get muddy. I was covered in mud and soaked from the rain. The mud was thick and heavy. You could wear it on the bottom of your shoe as a weight. My mom took me into the restroom to try and clean me up as best as she could. We were an hour or more from home so that wasn't an option to go home and change. I would have to watch Roy Clark with my hair and the rest of me covered in mud. To tell you the truth, somehow it didn't matter. I knew I would clean up just fine, but my bear would have been harder to get clean if he would have gotten muddy, not to mention that my mom probably wouldn't have allowed the bear in the house with mud on him. Not a stitch of mud got on him. So, he stayed clean and I was happy. Roy sang one of my favorite songs called: "Yesterday, When I Was Young". We went home right after Roy was done singing, and I smelled like a wet dog the whole way home.

As a teenager, I got to go with some friends of mine to a concert to see Bon-Jovi. The concert was fabulous and the opening band was Skid Row. I never listened to Skid Row until I saw them at this concert. I think Bon-Jovi made that band more famous. We had to drive to Hershey to see the bands, but it was well worth the ride.

Then in 1996, I met Richard Simmons at Wal-Mart on Benner Pike. I had Richard's exercise tapes and enjoyed listening to him. Richard was doing a talk and a book signing. He talked about his love for his Dalmatian dogs and tips on staying healthy and the importance of exercise. He signed one of his cookbooks called "Farewell to Fat". I wanted to ask him several questions but I was speechless. I finally asked him how to stay on track with my weight loss, and he handed me a wallet size commitment card to control your eating. He must have sensed my need to ask more, my lips wouldn't move, so he gave me a kiss on each cheek and moved on to someone else. Richard wore his sparkly tank top, shorts and sneakers. He smelled really good. Obviously, he hadn't been working out before he came to Wal-Mart. Richard didn't leave until he greeted every single person. He seemed to be a warm and caring person.

Later on in my life, around the 80s and 90s, I went to see Wynonna Judd, Ricky Martin, Tina Turner and The Kenny Rogers Christmas special at the Bryce Jordon Center. Around 2005 or so, I also saw in concert the "Rascal Flatts" band that put on a wonderful concert, also at the Bryce Jordon Center. Others I have also seen were Michael Fratleys, "Lord of the Dance", along with the Scottish Black Watch. They were fabulous, although I never had an opportunity to speak to any of these singers.

The last famous person I had met was a writer named, Tawni O'Dell. She wrote "Back Roads", which became a number one seller because of Oprah Winfrey's book pick. Tawni was on the Oprah show. Tawni has also written two other books, which I have read, and I had her sign all three. Tawni had given a talk about her book in State College in early 2007. She had said she moved from Allegheny County and has made State College her home now. Tawni's book, "Back Roads" will be out as a movie in 2008 or 2009.

One person I would like to have met was Michael Landon. His real name was Eugene Maurice Orowitz, born on Oct. 31, 1936. He died July 1, 1991 of pancreatic cancer. He was only 54 years old. He played "Little Joe" on the TV show Bonanza and later on in his life played in "Highway to Heaven" which he also starred. One of the shows all children liked to watch was, "Little House on the Prairie". I believe he was a good man and right before he died he had said something that has always stuck with me. He said; *"Somebody should tell us right at the start of our lives that we are dying. Then we might live life to the limit, every minute of every single day. Do it, I Say! Whatever you want to do – do it now! There are only so many tomorrows"*.

Another great legend was Elvis Presley. He was every girl's dream in his time. I don't think he will ever be forgotten. Unfortunately, Elvis died of an overdose of drugs. I guess fame just got the best of him.

A few people I would find interesting to meet are Barbara Walters and Anderson Cooper. Both have interviewed a lot of interesting people and have traveled to a lot of places just to get their stories. I find Jane Fonda interesting and love most of her movies and have a lot of her exercise tapes. I read her biography book about a year ago. As far as actors who I enjoy in film, they are: Tom Hanks, Mel Gibson and Nicolas Cage. Adam Sandler, Robin Williams and Drew Barrymore would be my comedy favorites. Some of the actresses in film I like are, Sandra Bullock, Jodie Foster and Brittany Murphy.

One of my all time favorite movies that I have watched over and over is called; "As Good As It Gets" with Jack Nicholson. Other movies that I like a lot are, "We Were Soldiers", "The Lake House", "Windtalkers", "FlightPlan" and "50 First Dates".

Ansel Adams is one of my favorite famous black and white photographers. I'm sure there are so many other famous actors, actresses, singers, writers and photographers that I am forgetting at the moment to mention. Whether I meet any of these people really doesn't matter, because I can enjoy what they produce and/or learn from them.

(Written November 2007)

The 60s and 70s

The 60s were a time when there were hippies, flower power, tie-dye shirts and things were groovy. President John F. Kennedy was shot while riding in his car in 1963. I was only three years old. I don't remember any of it, but I do remember watching reruns of that time on television. I think I would have liked him. Everything I have ever heard about him makes him seem like he was one of the great presidents. In 1967 the first heart transplant was performed and that was the same year as the first Super Bowl.

Back in the 60s, kindergarten wasn't mandatory and I never had to go. School always started in September and I was five years old when I started first grade. I would be turning six in November.

Growing up in the mid-to-late 60s, I had to watch black & white TV with three channels. The channels were ten (WTAJ), six (NBC) and three (PBS). Mostly we watched ten because it would come in the clearest. If we were to watch something on channel six and if it was fuzzy, my dad would get up on the roof and we'd yell up when the TV picture was clear. He would stand there and turn the antenna, sometimes even in the rain, which brought on yelling from my dad if he couldn't hear us. If only he could have stayed up there while we watched our shows, it would have been a lot clearer. Every-time my dad would let go of the antenna to come down off the roof; the picture would become fuzzy again.

When we moved in the early 70s, we got colored TV but still had the antenna. It wasn't till about the mid to late 70s that we got cable TV. The floor model was the way to go, and my parents still have that TV. The color in it isn't working so well, but to have to part with it, Oh My!

GI Joe and Barbie dolls were popular in the 60s, as well as one of my favorite TV shows, Sesame Street. It first aired in 1969. I was nine years old. A lot of kids loved Elmo and Big Bird, but my favorites are still The Grouch and Cookie Monster. "Puff the Magic Dragon" was a favorite of my youth, along with the TV show, "The Monkeys." Songs by the Beatles were number one, and girls would scream at their concerts and be in tears. I never could figure out why they had to cry. I say, nothing to cry about, but I was still young. I remember listening to the song, "The Yellow Submarine" on the radio. Everyone had to have a slinky, but I could never get mine to walk down stairs like the rest of the kids. The neighborhood girls would get together and ask our Magic 8 Ball questions. All you had to do was shake it after you asked a question and it would give you an answer. You just had to learn how to ask your questions the right way. There were only so many answers it would give.

Flowers were everywhere, along with people that would walk past you and hold up two fingers for the peace sign. I remember hearing about Woodstock in 1969, where a lot of hippies would go and listen to Rock & Roll and smoke pot. At least that's what was on the radio and the TV. The song San Francisco was popular with the lyrics saying: Where are you going with flowers in your hair? Also popular were Volks-Wagon (VW) vans and those cute Love Bugs. My sister, Janet, and I would play punch bug in the car. Every time you would see a VW, or a Beatle Bug car as they were called, you would punch the other person in the leg to see how much you could make it hurt. We would yell, "Ouch!" when getting hit. Then our mother would yell for us to stop it, and we would tell her we were just playing.

The 70s came rolling along when I was ten, and at the age of eleven, we moved from Raystown to across the fairgrounds in Huntingdon. My parents still live there. If we had to play indoors, Janet and I would play with our paper dolls for hours. Cut them out and dress them up in fancy clothes. After awhile they didn't stand very well. We also had a Rubik's Cube. The cube can become addictive sitting there for hours just trying to get those colors to match up on each side. When you got sick of trying, you could just take off the stickers and match them up. Then you couldn't play anymore because it would never be right again. Oh, and what about that Creepy Crawler bake set where you baked creepy bugs and the Hobby Easy Bake Oven? We would make the family a cake and make them eat it. I never thought they really wanted it. They all seemed a little bit scared to take that first bite. The snow cone maker seemed to be a lot safer, and no one seemed to mind taking a taste of that. I ordered Sea Monkeys from a catalog and then they sent them to me through the mail. Basically, they were sea horses. When it got dark, I would sit in my room and watch the Lava Lamp.

While riding the bus to school we would play with our Clackers. Clackers had two hard glass balls on the two ends of a string, and you would get them going fast enough to hit each other at the top of your arm. If you messed up, you would have a lot of bruises to show for it. A lot of kids on the bus would teach each other how to make towers and Jacob's ladders using string. You would put string on your hands and make different shapes out of them.

On nice sunny days, we would take our Hula Hoops out and wiggle our hips back and forth to keep them going. We also liked to play Chinese jump rope. Mostly we played that at school since the game took three people to play, one at each end and then one in the middle. Banana seat bikes were in, and you were really cool if you had a basket in the front. We had a game called Jarts. This was a lawn game with large darts, and you had to throw them up in the air and try to get them into a small hoop lying on the ground. They discontinued Jarts along with Clackers, as they were considered dangerous.

I got my first dog, a border collie named Ginger, and I had a favorite calico cat named Kitty. Kitty was named after Kitty on Gunsmoke. Kitty would follow Ginger and me around all day, and I would spend hours swinging on the porch swing with Ginger. When it was colder outside, Kitty would keep Ginger warm by lying on top of her. Ginger never minded it because it kept her warm. My mom never liked animals in the house.

17

My sister and I would argue over who liked Donny Osmond or David Cassidy better. I preferred David Cassidy who played on The Partridge Family. Bobby Sherman was another poster we had to have in our room hanging on the wall. My mom would sit in the evenings in front of the TV and watch Medical Center. She would say how good-looking Chad Everett was. I think her second choice was Chuck Woolery. He played on a game show called, "Love Connection." When a commercial would come up, he'd say; "be right back in two and two." All the girls liked Elvis Presley. The guys I think were jealous of Elvis and most would never admit that they liked him. While the girls had their favorites, the guys had their eyes on favorite stars like …hmm… well… I guess I wasn't paying attention to who the guys goggled over so you may have to ask them.

My dad preferred TV shows like Gunsmoke, Mash and Bonanza. I never minded watching Bonanza. I had a crush on Michael Landon who played Little Joe. Michael was good looking up till the day he died. Another program my dad liked was Kojak sucking on a lollipop and investigating those crimes. He liked a lot of western movies, including John Wayne.

Both my parents were into watching Hee-Haw on Saturday nights. I never cared for it when I was a teen but have grown to like the reruns as I have gotten older. I always liked Junior Sample with his car sales pitch and his BR549. Some of my parent's other favorite shows were "The Flip Wilson Show," "Lucy," and "Good Times" with J.J.'s Dynamite saying. The whole family liked watching "All In The Family" with Archie Bunker. My dad seemed a lot like Archie, and my mom could make a good Edith. The girls in our family would sit and watch "The Sonny & Cher Comedy Hour."

I remember my mom saying her favorite song was "Hey Jude". She loved that song. Richard, my brother, liked the song "Popsicle". It goes, "If you wanna keep cool, it does the trick and it comes on a stick". Richard's other favorite song was "American Pie." It would go like this,

18

"Bye, Bye, Miss American Pie, drove the Chevy to the levy but the levy was dry, and good ole boys were drinking whisky and rye, singing this will be the day that I die. And they were singing...Bye, Bye Miss American Pie." My sister, Janet, would try to sing to Cher with "Half-Breed" and Tina Turner songs like; "Proud Mary". I don't remember this song called "Tammy" by Debbie Reynolds but my sister said it was one her favorites. "I heard it through the Grapevine" was another one she liked a lot. I remember sitting on the couch one day with my cousin Diane and I were singing the song, "Let it Be". The song repeats itself a lot going..."Let it Be, Let it Be, Let it Be, Let it Be...These are words of wisdom, let it be..." etc. My sister got mad at us for singing it. Guess it started to drive her crazy and she came out to the living room from being in her bedroom and told us we sounded like a bunch of bees buzzing around. We couldn't sing it after that because we were too busy laughing.

In the late 70s, I was in my teen years. My sister and I would wear our mini-skirts, go-go boots and our mood rings. The mood rings changed colors with whatever mood you were in, although I don't remember what the colors mean anymore. We both tried our hand at putting makeup on our eyes with the blue eye shadow. I thought it looked really nice then, but now I am so glad it went out of style. We both liked our jewelry with our big hoop earrings and choker necklaces. I wore my hair long and straight with beads and a ribbon. I had my bangs feathered back for the Farrah Facet look. The song; "Hair"… long beautiful hair… shinning… gleaming…" etc. was popular on the radio. I got a record player one year for Christmas, and my sister and I played 45 and 78 rpms all the time.

When I was in high school, I had to make something in sewing class other than a pillow, so I made a pair of bell-bottom pants. I didn't like to sew then, and I still don't. I only ever wore them once. I was afraid the seams would come out, but the teacher said the thread would hold. When you wore your long bell bottomed pants, clogs were the shoes to wear so your pants didn't drag on the ground. Some of the guys liked those platform shoes and plaid pants. For our yearbook, everyone would pile into the phone booth to see how many people they could sardine in there and take pictures. When you got on the bus to go home, sometimes you'd pass someone streaking. This always brought on giggles from the girls. I only know of the guys who would run naked either by the bus or on some football field and have just their sneakers on. The song; "The Streak" was popular when this was going on. The lyrics go something like: And they call him the streak, fastest thing on two feet….etc. I don't think girls ever streaked then.

On the weekends, my sister and I would go to the dances at our local community center and hear songs like,"Knocking on Heaven's Door" and "Spiders & Snakes". Disco music was big then with the movie "Saturday Night Fever" with John Travolta; along with movies like Footloose and Flashdance. The 3-D glasses were popular with the movie, "The Birds". Our mom would drive my sister and me to go see other movies like; "Star Wars" and "Jaws". I don't remember my mom and dad ever going to the movies with us. The first VCR came out in 1971, but my parents never got one till sometime in the 80s. The blinking light flashed on the VCR till the 90s when they finally unplugged it. I tried to show them how to reset it but they never seemed that interested.

I passed my driver test at age sixteen and got my first car. My parents would never buy us a car, so I had to get a job. My first real job was working at a grocery store named "Riverside." I started out as a bag packer. I remember my car was blue and nothing to really look at so much to everyone else, but oh how I loved that car. I think it may have been some type of Oldsmobile. My parents were never big Ford fans. Everytime we got one something went wrong with it in a short period of time. I took care of my first car as if it were my baby. I added a troll with pink hair to put on my rearview mirror. Trolls were supposed to bring you luck. Guess I didn't have too much luck: my car broke down a year or so later, and I moved onto a Mustang. As with our luck with Fords, my mustang didn't run long. I think a mere six months. I sold it for $400.00 for the body and the tires. The motor blew up but someone had a motor they were going to put into it. I'm not sure why I remember how much I sold it for, but I do.

Some of the major events that were going on in the late 60s and part of the 70s were the United States fighting in the Viet Nam War. Then in 1974, Patty Hearst was kidnapped. I remember watching this all over the news. Patty was suppose to have been kidnapped and was forced to rob banks with her kidnappers. Later on, I heard that she fell in love with one of her kidnappers. I don't know what ever became of her. President Nixon resigned due to the Watergate scandal. Elvis Presley died in 1977. Everyone was saying the phrase; "Elvis has left the building".

As for me, my personal major events were in 1978. I graduated at the age of seventeen at the end of May. I was the only one in my family to walk down the aisle to pick up my diploma. My parents were proud of me, and so was I. My sister, and brother, both quit in high school. My sister got married, and my brother just hated school. I always felt that if you go all those years it would be stupid to quit in your last year. My parents never had the option to go to high school. They had to quit to help take care of their large families. My mom came from a family of fourteen siblings and my dad came from a family of eight siblings. My dad was in his late fifties when he studied for his GED. It was a proud moment and a great accomplishment for him. I had heart surgery right after graduation in 1978, and was in there for the Fourth of July at Cleveland Clinic in Cleveland, OH.

In 1979, I would marry my first husband (now an ex), along with having my first child, Lucas. And so it ends the 60s and 70s but will be a new beginning in the 80s.

The 80s and 90s will be another story....

Pound Puppy
(1989)

My two boys and I arrived at the dog pound looking for a small dog with not too much hair and one we all would like. I was divorced, so it seemed right that the boys should have their own dog. We took a look around and came across a little brown and white beagle mix that had the saddest look on his face. This was the one.

After we had gotten all the paperwork drawn up, and he was officially ours, the workers at the pound told us he was the one thousandth dog to arrive in their pound. They said this was the only thing that had saved this little dogs life, otherwise he would have been put to sleep. The problem was he had a bum leg and would kind of carry it instead of walking on it. This had made us want him even more. We knew he was what you'd called a "misfit" and not too many people would adopt a dog with a hurt leg, or anything else wrong with them.

The adventure began as soon as we got home. What a cute little dog. The boys got a phone call from the Humane Society asking if they would mind getting their picture taken with their new friend to help promote the dog pound. They were having an open house and wanted to put a big red ribbon on him. It even made it more exciting that this was their first dog. What young boy wouldn't be proud, and want their picture in the paper with their new friend? So, they said, "Yes!"

He ran around the car. Excited to be in a new home and to just be alive, we had to think of a new name for him. And since he was so fast to the point you could barely catch a glimpse of him from time to time, we would call him, "Flash". Yes, he was originally what you'd call a pound puppy. Flash was a spirited little dog. He loved running around with the boys, playing ball and sometimes just taking it easy. Flash's favorite time of the week was when we'd go to the bank. We'd go through the drive through and they always gave out little doggy treats and kid treats.

My children were given lollipops and Flash got a chew bone. All taken care of at the same time.

It was a sunny day, and the children were playing outside with Flash. My youngest son Mitch, about five years old came running to the house. He was out of breath and could hardly talk. He was yelling something, and I finally made out what it was. Baby Bear! Baby Bear! I ran out of the house knowing that if there was a cub somewhere there was surly the mamma bear around. My older son, Luke, who was around ten years old, was so scared of the bigger bear that he couldn't move. There was Flash barking and growling with all his might and saving my son. Flash distracted the bear enough that I could grab my son and take off for the house. We ran, and closed the door. The children were worried about Flash outside. After he knew we were safe he left the bear where she was and came barking at the door. We could see that no other name would have fit such a brave and fast little dog.

Later on when I met my husband, John, we moved to Bellefonte. When Flash would be in his dog box and the family would arrive home, he'd run around the box so fast you could barely see him, just like a bolt of lightning. Sometimes when he'd wiggle his way out of his collar he would run away for a few hours, but would always return at chow time.

When John and I would get Flash's leash to go for walks around the neighborhood, Flash would leap off the front step of our house like a horse jumping over posts. He would try to get as high as he could. I believe he knew we liked this, and he was always trying to please. He loved showing off his high jump.

Flash was a little mischievous at times, and he got into the neighbors flowerbed. He was digging, and rolling around in it. Maybe, he liked the fresh smell of flowers. The neighbor wasn't happy about it and we offered to make amends with new ones, but they decided they would grow back. They did indeed, and a few weeks later they had flowers blooming again, so all was well.

23

We decided to take Flash with us one day to Bald Eagle Park for a family walk. We didn't know how far the path went, but it seemed to take forever. When we finally got to the path along the water, Flash jumped in and just stood there because he was so hot and tired. Flash hated water, and for him to go even near it was a feat in itself.

I don't know what happened to Flash during his first two years of life, but I believe he gave our family the best ten. I feel he knew that we had rescued him, and was grateful that we come into his life. Toward the end of Flash's life he had his good days and bad days. Sometimes he could hardly walk or stand. At times he would fall, but the next day he would seem fine. We never knew what kind of day he was going to have, and we were undecided about what to do about it. It was an emotional decision we might have to make on whether to put him down, but I couldn't do it. Flash was twelve years old in dog years, but eighty-four in people years.

The one day when Flash was having one of his bad days he could hardly move, and this went on all day and into the evening. His bad days were more frequent now. I sat with him that evening and patted his head and told him it was okay for him to let go if he couldn't take it anymore. I told him the family would understand even though we would miss him. The next morning when we woke up he had passed away. I felt like he needed to be told to let go, like he was waiting for me to say our last good-byes. I don't know if he understood me, but with the turn of events, I feel like he did. I'd like to think so. He died either late Monday night on October 8, 2000, or early morning.

Maybe Flash didn't have nine lives like a cat, but he did get lucky. Sometimes, I think he knew that we saved him from sure death by picking him out at the Humane Society. The people there thought no one would want him because of his age and his hurt leg. How sad. But, how could his previous owners ever have given up such a loyal friend, and a good listener? That is something we will never know, but for us we were glad they did. How could we ever imagine how touched we would be by having that little dog come into our lives? Flash is sadly missed and thought of often.

Pound puppies may not be full-blooded or even ready to be a show dog with the most top-notch dogs, but you will never find a more devoted and loving dog. We had picked a winner!

If You Never Heard Of It
It Doesn't Necessarily Make It Strange

When I was in grade school, instead of each person bringing something for the teacher at Christmas, or at the end of the school year, we'd have a fruit roll. When teachers would turn their back to the class, one person who was assigned to the task, would stand up and yell, ROLL! We then would take out our piece of fruit and roll them down the aisles. Any piece of fruit that could roll was fair game, but mostly we brought oranges, apples, pears or grapefruits. As young students, I guess we never thought much about that dirty floor we were rolling them down, but I'm sure the teacher did.

My husband had never heard of it, so he figured it had to be one of those traditions that some "back woods" or "hick" school would do. Maybe he's right, I never heard of any other school districts doing this either, but it sure was fun watching the teacher's face when he or she saw a whole bunch of fruit coming their way. Our class always got a big kick out of it, as well as we didn't need to spend a lot of money on a gift. No one ever felt left out either, since we all had the same thing. The fruit sounded like thunder when the class rolled their fruit down the aisle in unison.

Other people found it strange about some of the meals our family would make when we were going through tough times. The cupboard would be just about bare and my mom and dad would say we were going to have one of our gourmet meals. The dishes were called, coffee soup and cracker soup. When making coffee soup, make black coffee, pour coffee over two slices of bread, put some sugar on it and you have coffee soup. As for cracker soup, this is done in a similar way only you put milk on some crumbled up crackers and add sugar to taste. It's an acquired taste, but my sister and I still make these dishes from time to time.

If you grew up in some big city like New York, Philadelphia or Pittsburgh, as my husband did, you possibly may not have heard about families hosting "Fresh Air Kids." My husband found the name of fresh air kids to be humorous simply because he thought I had a good imagination. He wondered why anyone would send their children away for two weeks to a family they didn't know, simply to get fresh air. I grew up in Huntingdon County, at Raystown. This area is now called Raystown Lake. We had a lot of fresh air and lots of areas to play without fumes from cars and smoke stacks from manufacturing plants. When my grandson reaches an age where he can play outside safely, I would like to host a fresh air child. I would be able to take them to Raystown Lake and let them swim in the crystal clear water. Some children have never seen wild animals or smelled the crisp air when it's about to rain. Sometimes you can even smell the earthworms. A lot of children would love to see a beautiful lake with lots of surrounding trees where they don't have to worry about getting hit with a car. I believe this is a great program for the children who have never gotten to be on a farm or smelled the air without fumes and/or smog.

Someone I had worked with once didn't know what a macadam was. He asked me if I knew and I told him; yes it's a paved blacktop road. I suppose the reason I found this one to be a little strange was because he had to drive to work everyday on a macadam road. I guess while growing up he just never knew the correct word for paved roads.

People from the Pittsburgh area find it a little strange, that around our area in Centre County we call our Pepsi or Coke, "soda." While in Pittsburgh they call it "pop." Some people in that area had thought, when we say soda instead of pop we were just being snobbish. When some of them got to know people from our area they realized it simply wasn't true. A lady from Virginia had told me where she grew up they simply called it a "soft drink". It just depended on how you were taught to say things or the area where you were born.

I used to call "carts" you use at the grocery store "buggies." That's what my mom always called them when we went grocery shopping.
When I came to Centre County, only an hour away, people thought it was strange that I would call a cart, a buggy. People used to tell me that a cart is for groceries and a buggy is to carry a baby in, so I changed what I called it. When you visit Huntingdon, you may hear people at the grocery store telling someone that they're with to put an item in their buggy.

I knew a guy from Huntingdon County, who didn't know what a BLT was. I found it to be strange, but it wasn't strange to him. I had to explain that a BLT was a bacon, lettuce and tomato sandwich. After eating one, he loved it.

When we are unaware of things and simply do not know, it doesn't mean we are ignorant or dumb. It also doesn't make it strange. It just may mean that it was how we were brought up as children or the area we lived in. What one person finds strange, you may find normal.

Michelle

I was doing my photo- a-day blog and one of the bloggers posted ten questions for me to answer. The one question I have been thinking about was; "Who is, or was, your best friend, and why?" My best friend went to high school with me. We went to dances together, went on a diet together, and told each other our secrets and knew we would each keep them. Michelle was my best friend.

After graduation, I went to The Cleveland Clinic for my heart surgery. Michelle wrote to me almost every day so I'd be kept up on all the news, along with sending me articles from my hometown newspaper. The town was having a fundraiser to help with the surgery expenses. I was in a room with four other girls and at night it always felt like we were at a slumber party. We would stay up half the night getting to know each other. That didn't keep me from wanting to hear from Michelle, who knew me best. There wasn't anything we couldn't tell each other.

I was seeing my soon-to-be husband at the time and Michelle had just married Brian. His parents and Michelle never seemed to get along because according to Michelle she wasn't the right faith of religion. Brian and Michelle were always at odds with each other over this. I tried to talk Michelle out of marrying him, but they ended up marrying anyway. I'm not sure why I didn't attend, because we had promised each other we would be each other's maid-of-honors. It may have been around the time of my surgery.

I was soon married (to whom would later become my ex). One week I had been talking to Michelle and we were making plans to go on a double date. A week later, I got the bad news that Brian shot her the same Saturday we were suppose to go out together. I don't remember what came up but we had to cancel. I think my son had gotten sick at the time and he was just a baby.

Michelle's husband had shot her on Piney Ridge, while in her vehicle. I heard he was ramming her car with his car and she finally decided to stop. When she did, he shot her and drove off. After he shot Michelle he went to his parents house, went upstairs and shot himself. There wasn't too much about it in the paper.

I know Michelle loved Brian and knew she would never have gone out with someone else. I couldn't imagine that anything could have been that wrong that they couldn't have worked it out.

I regret that I didn't go to the funeral. I couldn't do it. I was overcome with fear, seeing her in a coffin. I had a hard time dealing with funerals ever since my favorite grandmother died. I had to go then but I had a hard time with it. I wish I had gone. I still feel like I didn't pay my respects and she was my best friend.

I suffered from bad dreams for months afterward with Michelle speaking to me in my dreams. Later on, they got less and less. I wish many times that Michelle was still around to laugh with, and I miss how we used to talk to each other for hours whether on the phone or visiting each other. It's amazing how one question can trigger so many memories.

Michelle is sadly missed.

Out of Breath

I had asthma really bad as a child. When I was around six years old, I stopped breathing. I went into my mom's room to sleep in her bed because I was scared and that's when it happened. My mom didn't know CPR so she kept shaking me till I came back around. It's a good thing I slept in her bed or she wouldn't have known that I stopped breathing. I also know now that I was lucky that her shaking me helped that day.

In the early teen years it seemed that I had "outgrown" my asthma, but I would soon find out in my early twenty's it would return from a gas tank leak that had been buried in the ground underneath a gas station. The smell had gotten so bad that the Department of Environmental Resources had to come and order the gas station to dig up the tanks and remove them. I had a "country" doctor and he said you never really "out grow" it. It becomes dormant until something triggers it back. Usually, something from the environment triggers it, which was the case for me.

While in my teen years my parents thought that I was getting my asthma back because I was getting out of breath. Even walking up a hill, walking longer periods of time, and running short distances I would become out of breath. I told my parents I didn't think it was asthma because it was different.

When I had an asthma attack I had a hard time breathing at night and it felt like my lungs couldn't expand to let air into them. When you have an asthma attack your bronchial tubes start to close and get twisted and the opening becomes smaller so you can't get air into them. I knew that this was different because I was huffing and getting out of breath even walking on flat services for long or sometimes shorter distances. But, this would go away after I would stop walking or running around and calm down. With asthma I'd only get relief through my medication.

After complaints became more frequent my parents decided that they better start to get it checked out by the doctors. I started to see a doctor for this when I was around fourteen years old. The first doctor we went to had said I had a heart murmur, which a lot of people could have and not even know it. This doctor said I should just wait for about a year and get a checkup again to see if it would improve or get worse.

My next checkup at fifteen was more of a concern and the doctor sent me to Altoona Hospital for more testing. I had a cauterization there. That's where they put a tube in your vein with a balloon type ball on the end of it. When the catheter is placed where they want it, the balloon end can inflate to take pictures. They went up through my arm and wiggled it to where it needed to be to reach my heart area. While they do this you have to drink some type of chalky stuff that seems to start from the tip of your head to the bottom of your feet. It's warm going through your body and you can feel where it is at in your body while it travels down. Some doctors go up through the leg but I was glad they did it going through my arm. To me it seemed like a shorter distance.

After about a week I found out that they felt I would need heart surgery for a hole in my heart. The hole was the size of a half-dollar as they described it. That left only two chambers in my heart working instead of four. Since Altoona hospital didn't do this kind of major heart surgery at the time, they told me they would send me to Cleveland Clinic in Ohio. Altoona hospital told me this was one of the best facilities besides Hershey. Hershey at the time was pretty booked up. The doctors said I could wait till after graduation to have my surgery.

While I was in school my junior and senior year, I wasn't allowed to participate in heavy running or gym class that was a strain on me. Finally, a year later in 1978, I graduated and was scheduled for heart surgery in Cleveland toward the end of June and into July. I went to graduation at the end of May and by the end of June I was on my way to Cleveland with my parents to have surgery. I was only seventeen and going to be having major heart surgery. I was never really terrified of surgery because I was a teen, and just trusted the doctors that they wouldn't make a mistake.

Cleveland was a really nice hospital with a lot of excellent doctors in specialty fields. The doctors told me when I got there that they never take another hospital's test results as confirmation, so I had to repeat the cauterization test. They also like to double-check the exact location before operating. I was allowed to watch the cauterization on a TV screen, which proved to me that this surgery was indeed necessary. It was just a bit uncomfortable to see my vein cut, but I thought it was "cool" to watch the procedure.

The doctors confirmed that I would indeed need the surgery. I asked them, "What happens if I don't have the surgery?" Dr. Hodgeman, the heart specialist explained the risks of no surgery would mean a shortened life span to be around the age of forty. If I had kids, he said I would most likely die in the delivery room. Well, at that point I saw no other choice. So I was going to have the surgery.

The doctor explained to me that all babies are born with holes in their hearts at birth and they normally close as you grow older, however, mine kept increasing in size. He explained to me that they would use a patch and some wire to close the hole in my heart. They prepped me for surgery and had to give me injections in each leg to keep me from moving. It had scared me because I thought they had paralyzed me. They explained it would wear off after the three-hour surgery was over.

After the surgery, I was put in recovery and later I was moved into a room with four other girls around my age. They ranged from fourteen to eighteen years old. The nurses had to help me get up out of bed because when I tried to get up myself it felt like someone was ripping my chest open with a crowbar. I had to push around an IV pole and a blood container that kept the blood transfusing into my body. The nurses kept me walking the halls because the doctor said I needed to keep my lungs expanded.

After surgery your lungs can collapse so you have to exercise to keep them from collapsing. After around four days or so when they knew I wasn't going to need the wire that was attached to me from my insides to the outside they needed to take it out. They came into my room and the doctor pulled on it slowly to remove it. While he is doing this I could feel the wire as it left my body. A strange feeling because I felt like it was getting caught on one of my organs. The wire seemed longer than I thought it would be and I was glad when it was over. All the nurses wanted to see the doctor pull it out and asked my permission to watch. I had about five nurses standing around me watching the procedure. If I remember right, the wire is inserted incase after surgery I would go into cardiac arrest. This would help revive me easier. Luckily, I didn't need it.

After about a week, the nurses kept me walking the halls, and when I could walk down the hall myself they would let me do it without tagging along. I remember being in there over the Fourth of July and was disappointed that I couldn't see the fireworks. Our family always watched the fireworks on a hill above our house. The girls, who were in the same room as me, we all started talking, laughing and getting to know each other. Wearing our pajamas all the time made it seem we were having a slumber party.

The other girls weren't in there for the same surgery as mine. The one girl, named Rhonda, had blonde straight hair and was in there for a breast reduction. She was having a lot of back pain. The one girl whose name I can't remember, looked like a model with dark hair, very pretty, she was there for a hysterectomy. She was disappointed that she wouldn't ever be able to have kids and figured she would adopt someday. Julie, another girl, had dark hair, tall and slender, but I don't remember why she was there.

The girls and I used to walk down the hall and play pool. The hospital had a pool table and a game room for the teenagers. We were always there when we didn't have to be in our rooms. If one of our parents were with us we could get dressed and walk down to the snack bar. This was a big deal for us. Between the four of us we were always lucky enough to have one adult there when we needed one. We could also get dressed and go outside the hospital grounds. I really enjoyed walking outside since I was cooped up for a week. I was in the hospital about two weeks. As the girls started to leave, we promised each other we would write and keep in touch with each other. We exchanged addresses and did keep in touch for about two years. After that we slowly stopped writing and lost touch with each other.

I was being released and packed up my belongings and headed back to Pennsylvania with my parents. Before I left the hospital, Dr. Hodgeman said, I needed to walk everyday at least one mile, preferably two miles everyday to keep my lungs expanded and to keep them from collapsing. Dr. Hodgeman said my lungs needed to be strengthened and get stronger.

When I got back home, I found out that the community had all my updates from my surgery in the paper and had a fundraiser for me to collect money to help out with the doctor and hospital bills. An insurance agent named Joe Champa, was a member of the Kiwanis club who had started the fundraiser. My parents also dealt with him because they had car insurance through him. He was a very polite man. My parents insurance wouldn't cover the cost of all the bills that had accrued. The Kiwanis Club ended up raising about $3, 500.00 to put toward the bills. It was overwhelming to see that this was happening and that so many people I didn't even know cared enough to do this.

After a few months of being home, the Kiwanis wanted me to come speak to the club because they had done so much work. They wanted me to give them an update on my surgery and my experience in the hospital. My dad took me there because the Kiwanis is only a group for men. I was more nervous speaking in front of all those men than I was having the surgery. That was my first speech at the age of seventeen.

I did keep up with the walking for about two years after surgery and went back for a yearly checkup, then a five year checkup, and then periodically. My last regular checkup was around 1995 and they told me I wouldn't need to come back unless there was a problem, which they didn't foresee any. They gave me a clean bill of health as far as my heart goes. My heart doctor retired about a year after my last checkup, and I haven't been back since.

Heart problems run in my family. In 2004 my dad had surgery at the VA hospital in Altoona, PA for a blockage in his heart. He is fine now, which was when he was the age of seventy-four. My uncle, Robert "Bob" Cresswell, my dad's brother, had an artificial heart and was the first person to survive one year with this device. Penn State University in State College, PA had built the artificial heart for him. They could not find a donor match in time, and he died in Hershey, PA without ever getting a heart transplant. And, recently (2007), my mom had a massive heart attack.

Over the years I have done family research and found out that heart problems have a history of taking the lives of my family members, and I will have to make sure my children and grandchildren keep getting regular checkups for this kind of problem.

My heart is fine now, but I live with allergy-induced asthma and will the rest of my life. There is no cure for asthma and my new doctor who treats asthma and allergies said they haven't come very far with a cure for this kind of lung disease. He said it hasn't changed that much as far as the medications they use or the research they have done in about the last thirty-five to forty years. I just have to hope that I don't get as bad as my one cousin, Judy, who has to sleep under an oxygen tent at night. Hopefully, there will be a cure in the future. But until then, just like I have been doing for the last five years, I will keep getting my allergy shots every week. The shots have definitely helped me.

Embarrassing Or Funny
(Depending On How You Look At It)

Have you ever had those embarrassing moments when you thought you'd like to crawl away and hide? Or, did you laugh at someone else with something you thought was funny? It depends on whose side you're looking at it whether you were embarrassed and red faced, or was the one doing the laughing. Depending on which side your on, you may think these are either funny or embarrassing. What would you have done?

In1992 I was dating John, who would later become my husband. We were still in the first dating stages and I wanted to impress him. What was about to happen I don't believe impressed him, at least not in a good way. I had been at his house with my younger son Mitch, to surprise him by cooking him a lovely dinner. Mitch and I both had used the bathroom facilities and when I was done I flushed. It was clogged and the water was rising fast. I was praying it would stop, and thankfully it did at the rim of the bowl. I looked everywhere for a toilet plunger but there was none to be found. I did the only thing I could, since my car was broke down, my son and I had to walk back to my house to get my plunger. The walk was about ten blocks away in Bellefonte.

We got back to my house, got the toilet plunger, and headed back to Johns place. Mitch and I were both embarrassed walking through Bellefonte with a plunger in hand. My son just kept telling me to walk faster. I didn't tell him, but that was fine with me. It was embarrassing enough walking with that thing in broad daylight, but then the worse happened. There was John driving by in his car. I was hoping he wouldn't spot us, but he did. I wanted to become an ostrich and bury my head in the sand. He turned the car around and came back and asked the dreaded question; "why do you have a toilet plunger with you walking downtown?" I explained. He offered us a ride back to his place even though we were half way there. We were married a year later in 1993.

One day, in 1998 we decided to go bowling. We had gone bowling before, but again this would turn out to be an embarrassing moment for me. I was bowling fairly well, although I am not an expert, so when I say fairly well, I mean for me. We were playing our second game when my thumb got stuck in the ball as I threw it. I went down the aisle with the ball. I felt like a tree and someone yelling: TIMBER!

All I could do was lie there. I was visualizing different ways to get up gracefully. I felt like there was a clock in front of me and all I could hear was the ticking. After what seemed like an hour, but it was probably less than a minute, I decided there was no way to get up gracefully. It just wasn't going to happen that way. I stood up and looked around to see who might have seen me falling. I started to laugh and pretend I did it on purpose. I saw two people looking at me and they chuckled to themselves, but weren't really laughing. A few others just looked away when I glanced their way.

My husband knew I didn't fall on purpose and wanted to burst out laughing, but he didn't until he saw I was okay. He looked like a statue standing there in awe. I brushed myself off and looked at him and laughed. Then he let the laughter loose. He said; I would have laughed at him if he had done that. And, yes it's true; I would have, so I was okay with it. I'm sure there are other moments in my life that I was embarrassed about, but these are the ones that seem to stand out. When reminiscing they are brought up from time to time, but in a lovingly teasing way.

John, however, had his moments as well. Sometime in the year 2000, my husband and I went to Pittsburgh to see his parents. We went outside to take a leisurely stroll. John and I came upon this road that had a wire across it about two feet off the ground. I decided to go around it since there was an opening on either side. He decided to show off and jump over it. When he jumped, his foot got caught and he fell right on his hands and fractured his wrist. He was embarrassed to go to the hospital, but I took him anyway. It took his wrist several weeks to heal. Not one of his better moments.

I have heard about and/or witnessed embarrassing moments from other people as well.

Janet, my sister, had her embarrassing moment when I was visiting one day around 1998. Her husband had a large fish tank where they kept a three-foot eel. They had a cover on the tank, but the eel pushed his way out of the tank and fell to the floor. My sister didn't know how to get it back it the tank because if you touched it, it would bite. She decided to get a fish net that they used when they go fishing in Canada. The fish net looked much bigger than the eel. The net was huge. She looked like a fisherman in her own living room. It would have been funnier if she had put on the fishermen boots. Oh well, can't have everything. All I could do was laugh while watching her try to get this large eel in a net to get it back in the tank. It kept flopping all over the living room floor. As she would try to scoop it up, it would flop toward her, then she would jump about a foot in the air. Finally, she did however get it back it the tank. I never laughed so hard about anything except when Delmar told his story.

While working at Corning, around 1988, I was working with a friend named Delmar. We worked on panel side as inspectors. He started to tell us about a time when he was house sitting one of his friends home, while he was out of town. While checking on the house, Delmar took along his dog, and another friend. Suddenly his dog came bounding in the house with the owner's prize-winning rabbit. Delmar and his friend were worried about how upset this man would be, so they came up with a plan. The plan was to wash off the prize rabbit, blow dry it, and put it back in the cage so the owner would think it died of natural causes. The dog left no marks on the rabbit anywhere, so they thought they were safe. When the owner came home he had gone outside to check on something. When he came back in, he looked at Delmar and his friend and said; "there are some sick people around here." Delmar asked him, "why?"

39

The owner of the house said to Delmar, that two days before he had gone on vacation his rabbit died and that some sick person dug up his prized rabbit, washed it off, put it back in its cage and closed the door. Delmar and his friend just looked at each other trying not to laugh until they got out of there. At Corning that day we couldn't stop laughing as we kept chuckling to ourselves. I have told that story many times as it was the funniest I've ever heard. *(No one tells this story better than Delmar.)*

Other stories will be added from time to time, as they come back to me while reminiscing, telling stories that I have heard or have seen, just like they will be telling stories about me.

Bunny in Our Backyard

Family Reunions

When I was growing up our family would always go to the Baker family reunion. My mom came from a family of fifteen children. Including all the aunts, uncles and cousins, there would be over sixty people at the gathering. My mom used to go every year until her mom died. After that, she went about once every six or seven years. It's a shame because I stopped going too, and I don't know half of my cousins now or what they are doing.

I got to thinking about this recently and decided that next year (2008) I would like to go to the reunion. Every first Saturday of July they get together. The children play games. They play the sack game where two people put one foot in the sack and you tie yourself to that person. Whoever goes past the finish line first, wins. The egg race is popular also. On this game, you take an egg and put it on a spoon and run as fast as you can without dropping the egg. The person who still has their egg intact at the finish line wins. They give away small prizes. There are other games, some for the adults.

Every family brings a dish, and there is plenty of food to share. No one goes away hungry. While eating you can catch up on the latest news from all the relatives. You hear laughter and people reminiscing about the past. The reunion goes on all day while the children play and the grown-ups talk. An auction is held in the afternoon. This is a lot of fun to see what everyone brings. You can bring a new item or one that was used. Sometimes people will try to figure out what the heck someone was thinking when donating the item. It's just fun. The money goes toward the picnic area rental and to send out postcard invitations for the following year.

Later when the sun goes down, everyone watches old reel movies from years gone by. You get to see what you were like when you were younger, the arguments on tape, and the people who have passed away. Then it's off to BBQ hotdogs and hamburgers for the evening while enjoying leftovers.

After a long day of fun activities, it's time to go home. Most of these relatives will not see each other for another year. I haven't gone to a family reunion for at least eight years, and I am hoping to get to know my relatives again. I miss them.

Pap and Gram Baker

Gram and Pap Cresswell

My grandmother Cresswell, on my dad's side of the family would baby-sit my sister and I when we were around eight to ten years old. She would take walks with us and when it would rain, she'd let us jump right in the mud puddles and get all wet and dirty. Gram used to tell us we are kids and that's what kids do. It was amusing to her to let us get all dirty from the mud knowing that my dad and mom would be all upset when they came to pick us up. Now that I'm older I think she just wanted to live life without making it seem so complicated, and not wanting to follow the rules that other people thought we should live by.

In the evenings, my grandmother would sit and watch TV shows like Mission Impossible. I can remember the theme music coming on for the show, then the striking of the match, it lighting, and then you'd see the fire going down a rope. Some of the other shows she watched were things like Kojak, game shows and sometimes soap opera's.

The hobby she loved most was playing bingo, and she would go and play at least once a week, sometimes twice. My mom and dad would take us kids along on Saturdays when they played, and we would run around outside having a good time. We would play hide and seek, and now and then go in to get some money for some soda, candy or a bag of chips.

I also remember my Gram sitting for hours at a little card table doing puzzles. I never could understand why this was so exciting for her, but that was one of her passions. I think about it now, and it probably was the love of a good challenge. She would have called it; "brain power."

I don't remember my grandfather Cresswell interacting with us children much, but do remember him as being tall and slender. During the last few years of his life he was in a wheel chair. I don't know why or how he became to be wheel chair bound. He had lung problems and he would take a big heaping spoonful of Vicks and eat it. I would cringe at the thought of this every time I seen him taking a bite. He'd have a jar sitting close by on a side table with a spoon resting on the lid.

I never ate Vicks, but I can remember my mom rubbing it on my chest when I was young. She'd say it would help get rid of my colds faster. It didn't smell too bad, but I can remember the warmth it gave off as I fell to sleep. I couldn't image the heat going down my throat to my lungs as my grandfather had done.

My grandfather died before I was a teenager, but I don't remember exactly when. However, because my grandmother and I were close, I do remember her dying on New Years Day. I have always hated New Years. I come to realize, as I had gotten older that the reason this is one of my worst holidays, (and probably the only holiday I dislike,) is because that's when she died. She was a special lady in many ways and will always be remembered.

Gram and Pap Cresswell

My First Four Jobs

Introduction: I have changed the names of the owners (Mr. and Mrs. Buck) of the restaurant to conceal their identities. I have also changed all the names of my co-workers (my fourth job) that were involved with this story. (The story, however, is true.) I want to talk about one job in particular my fourth job, but feel I need to give a brief description of my first three jobs first.

Just like most young girls, my first job was a babysitting. I babysat my two nieces, ages five and six, while my brother and his wife went to work. Everyone thought they were twins since they were only one year apart. I loved playing with the girls since I was only twelve or thirteen years old at the time myself. I would ride bikes with them, take them sled riding, read to them and dress them up so I could practice my photography. I loved to take pictures and had since around ten years old. I always spent the money on toys for them or to get photos developed, so I didn't really consider this a real job. But, technically it was my first paying job.

My second job, and to me a "real job" because I got to go out of the house, lasted three hours. I started to work at a truck stop as a waitress. I hated it! I made a dollar and ten cents an hour, plus tips. The truck drivers would come in and make sexual comments and try to grab your behind. No matter how much you'd tell some of them not to do it, they kept it up like it was funny. The only ones enjoying my misery were them. I wasn't good at handling this situation, so after three hours, I walked out the door. I quit and never went back for my paycheck. I figured it wasn't worth it.

At age seventeen, I graduated and had heart surgery. After my recovery, I got my third job. I worked as a bag packer at Riverside in Huntingdon. Training was easy. Put the can goods on the bottom, bread and eggs on top. After one hour, or even before that, you should know what you're doing. I didn't mind it as it got me my first car. I don't remember the make of the car, but I do remember it was blue and an older model. I got my first real job and my first car at seventeen. My parents wouldn't buy my sister, brother, and me a car, we had to work for it. It wasn't much to look at, but it was mine, and I was proud of it. I would wash that car and keep it clean like it was some car in a beauty pageant. My parents and siblings would laugh at me but I didn't care. She was a beauty in my eyes. I don't remember what ever happened to it, it must have just run out of steam.

The other benefit of having a job at Riverside was I got a discount card for the store Penn Traffic. I loved to shop there because I found clothes that weren't like everyone else's. I found a white sweater with blue trim going down the front sides and around the bottom. I had never seen another person wearing a sweater like that one. I quit when I got married to my first husband at age nineteen. I think that's when I lost my favorite sweater in the shuffle of the move.

My fourth job I started after my first-born son, Lucas, was around six months old or so. I was 20 years old. My husband (at that time) wasn't working or was between jobs so I decided to go to work. He never got a year-round job, because he always wanted to work somewhere so he could have part of the year off, like working construction. But, that's another story, and I won't go there right now.

Anyway, I got a job working at a respectable restaurant. It definitely wasn't a truck stop. The restaurant was more of a family style restaurant. My Aunt Stella worked there and showed me the ropes. Stella showed me her method of getting good tips. Aunt Stella would flirt with the men and then after a little flirting conversation with the guys, she would turn to the ladies of the table and give them a wink. She said this showed them it was all in fun since you don't want to piss off the ladies. If you make them mad you know you're not getting a good tip even though the guy may be paying. I never could really do that gesture. It wasn't me and felt unnatural. So, I decided just to rely on my own personality by being nice to everyone at the table and giving them good service. I didn't do too badly with the tips, although I must admit, Aunt Stella did get a lot more.

The owners came across as good Christian people who went to church every Wednesday and Sunday. They never missed. But, I would soon learn that they didn't treat their employees like they were Christians. The owner, Mr. Buck would hit on the girls behind his wife's back. The wife, Mrs. Buck, would cut back on your hours if she felt something irritated her or if she wanted someone else to work there that week. She didn't care if you had been there longer and did a better job. One day a girl I worked with named Patty had gotten a call from her scared four year old that the babysitter didn't show up. But, Mrs. Buck on purpose decided not to tell Patty because she needed her at work. Patty had a bad feeling about fifteen minutes after Mrs. Buck got the phone call and Patty called home to find out her four year old was home alone. She quit that day. I don't blame her. Before that incident, several weeks earlier, Patty was drinking a coffee and eating her meal on her off time. She was getting ready to work but didn't need to punch the time clock for another half an hour. Mrs. Buck said it was getting busy and told Patty to go to work right now. Patty told her as soon as she was done, as she had paid for her meal. I had seen Mrs. Buck grab the food and drink from in front of Patty and toss them down the food disposal. I couldn't believe it, but Patty still went to work after she did that. But, when it came to her child that was the last straw.

Mr. Buck would go behind his wife's back and tell you at the end of your shift if you'd make it worth his while, he'd help you clean up. He said that to me one day, and I told him, I'll clean it myself and to leave me alone. I know of only one girl who had worked there that ever had an affair with him and he would go to her house. The "Bucks" son Ben worked in the kitchen. I don't think he ever knew. If he did, he never mentioned it. We always got the impression from him that his parents were in the right with anything they did and they had good reasons to do them. As far as breaks…well…what breaks? If you tried to take a break, they were always behind you telling you to get back to work. So, breaks were few and far between.

Mrs. Buck decided one day she wanted one of her relatives to work there and cut back hours on a friend of mine named, Jen. Jen wasn't the only one, Mrs. Buck cut back my hours too. We ended up with around eighteen hours and the new person had a full time job. Well, enough was enough. You can only take so much. Jen and I came up with a plan. We decided that the next time we were scheduled to work together and there was no one else in there except the cook, we were quitting. It couldn't have worked out any better. We got scheduled on a Friday evening. Friday's were really busy. We waited until the first shift left and then around 5 p.m. the crowd started to arrive for dinner. We took our aprons off, told Ben (the only cook working at the time) that we were quitting. The restaurant was full and Ben begged us to stay. We told him his parents always treated their employee's like dirt, and we walked out the door. Mission accomplished. Ben knew we were leaving because of the hours, mistreatment, no breaks, but we didn't have the heart to tell him about his wandering dad. Maybe he knew already and just didn't want to admit it.

I know it may not have been right to take it out on the son, and yes it did suck for Ben, but we wanted to get back at his parents. Ben had to be waiter, cook, and dishwasher until someone arrived to help. If his parents had treated employees with the respect they deserve, then it wouldn't have had to end with Jen and me leaving that way. Mr. and Mrs. Buck were messing with our livelihood by cutting hours, I had a baby at home, and not to mention bills and a husband I was taking care of. Jen and her husband had bought a house. At least if anything went wrong with Mr. and Mrs. Bucks restaurant business, they had rental units to fall back on. We had nothing. At this point though it wasn't worth the stress.

A year or so later, the restaurant closed down because they couldn't keep employees. No wonder. And by the way, I filed for unemployment. I was denied at first because I quit. Then I filed an appeal. It was up to me to prove just cause to get unemployment from this job. When the hearing came before what they called a referee for employment compensation, I presented my case. I typed up a written document of everything they did to their employees. I also had Jen, Patty and my husband testify in my behalf. Jen told of no breaks and what they did to Patty. Patty was there to tell her own story and my husband was there just to tell them how upset I'd be after work when I got home. Sometimes I got so frustrated I'd be in tears. Mr. Buck and his son, Ben, showed up to represent their side. Mrs. Buck never showed up. Ben got mad at me for talking about his mom when she wasn't there. I told him to go get her, I'd gladly tell her to her face. Then Mr. Buck and Ben tried to delay the hearing by saying they didn't know I'd have all those witnesses and they didn't have any. I said to the referee they had just as much time to prepare as I had. He agreed, so we proceeded.

I won my unemployment, and was informed that they had had other complaints from previous workers in the past. I have had a lot of jobs, but I'd have to say the Buck's were the worst employers I ever worked for. Jen, Patty, and I always wondered, how could people claim to be Christians and treat people this way?

The lesson here is: *Treat other people the way you want to be treated.*

The Corn Maze
And
Pumpkin Patch

October 2nd, 2005. What did we do for our anniversary? John and I shared it with Landon. This was our grandson's first corn maze. It seemed exciting for a two and a half year old and it was our first corn maze as well. We decided to go to J.B. Tree Farm, which is located in Alexandria, PA, near Huntingdon where I grew up. Landon was excited and he knew he'd get to pick out his very own pumpkin.

We arrived and as we opened the door you could feel the excitement. It was a hot summer day, and the sun was glaring down upon us, but it didn't matter how hot it was because by the entrance was real reindeer. As Landon reached out his hand along the fence line he yelled, "Wow! Reindeer! Just like Santa's!"

We told Landon we'd see them on the way out and headed toward the corn maze. As we started to pass a few bails of hay, I stopped to get a photo of Landon with Pap. What a wonderful picture and I knew that would be a scrapbook page for me later on. We paid for our tickets to get into the maze and headed out.

We went up one way and then had to turn around and come back to try another way. This went on for a good while and after about and hour and a half we still couldn't find our way out. Landon had a worried look on his face and figured we'd never get out of there. He didn't realize we could just walk out when we wanted to.

As the day was nearing afternoon the temperature got up in the high eighties and the sun was beating down on us. Landon walked about fifteen minutes of the time spent in there and John and I took our turns carrying him, although John did most of the carrying. Landon started to get red faced and tired and just wanted out of there. We were all dry-lipped and thirsty. Water…Water! Landon weighed around thirty pounds and carrying that much weight your arms feel like they are about to break.

Finally, we came upon an emergency exit door, just made for people like us, people who can't find their way through a maze and have had enough. We took the opportunity to exit. Once you go out the gate there is a short dirt path to the beginning where the gift shop is located and the parking area.

We got our bottled water from the gift shop and I asked Landon if he wanted to pick out his own pumpkin. He said, "I don't want to leave without it." So, we headed for the great pumpkin patch. This would be another photo opportunity for me. We loved watching Landon's face light up as he tried to decide the best pumpkin to go home with. It's really a joy to watch children as they see things for the first time and it makes you feel you're living a new adventure through their eyes. It can make you feel like a kid again.

We had about an hour drive to get home and Landon was so excited and kept looking at his pumpkin. He didn't fall asleep in the car, which is usually what he does on long car rides. Landon never was much for taking naps, and like most kids who do take naps, well… Landon is not one of them.

51

When we got home we figured Landon would be excited to get his hands in all that gunk in that pumpkin and pull all the seeds out. Wrong we were. Landon said he didn't want to get his hands messy. I ended up taking the seeds out of the pumpkin for him and Pap drew a few pictures of scary faces for Landon to pick from so we could carve it out. Drawing the faces and letting him choose which one would be carved out made him feel important.

I washed the seeds, salted them and put them in the oven for about an hour on 250 degrees. Landon thought they tasted like popcorn.

Next October Landon will be a year older and we'd like to take him on a hayride. He will again pick out his own pumpkin; however, we will wait a few years to do a maze again. The carving will still have to be done by us but Landon doesn't seem to mind. Maybe he'll even get his hands a little dirty to do his own pumpkin cleaning. Until next year…

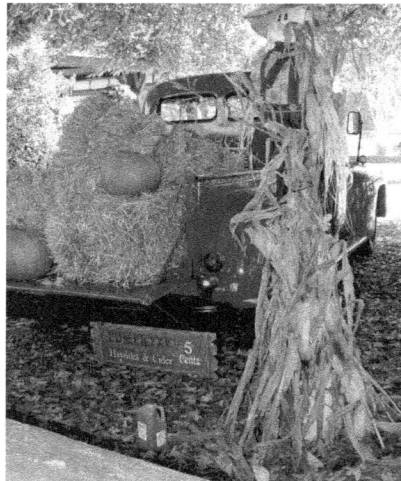

Hayrides and Pumpkins

The Road Leads To Parris Island
(2003)

Mitch, my youngest son graduated from Huntingdon Area High School in 2003. He had attended Bellefonte and Huntingdon schools, but went to Huntingdon part of his last year. Mitch was having some difficulty with a teacher and thought it was best to finish out his senior year in Huntingdon. He stayed with his dad while there. After graduation he returned home to Bellefonte.

Mitch wanted to join a branch of the military. He had talked to the Army, Air Force and the Reserves but finally decided he wanted to become a Marine. The Marine recruiter came to talk to my husband and me to see what we thought about Mitch joining the military. If Mitch would have had doubts, I would have too, but it was his dream and that's all he had talked about for three years. So, I had no objection to him joining. I told the recruiter I had no problem with it even though sometimes I would be scared to death. My husband, John, had been in the Army from 1985 to 1988 and had talked to Mitch about some of the things he had experienced just to make sure he knew what he was getting himself into.

Mitch signed up for the Marines for four years full time (active) and the Marines make them sign a contract for an additional four years for the reserves. He would be eligible to leave active duty in August of 2007. He would then spend another four years till August of 2011 during which he could get called up again. Mitch's friend signed up for the Marines and left for Parris Island sooner. They wanted to go together, but that didn't happen.

Mitch left in August of 2003 on his dad's birthday to train at Parris Island, S.C. The recruiter picked him up at the house and took him to the Harrisburg airport. When Mitch arrived in Washington, DC, he decided to get a bite to eat before his next plane was to leave. This was Mitch's first time going to an airport by himself. The only other time he had flown was on a trip to Florida with the family when he was only ten years old. When he was done eating he went to the boarding gate. He figured he had made it because he had a few minutes to spare, but the plane had already left. They told him that he needed to be there at least fifteen minutes before the plane takes off and they told him last call was five minutes ago. Mitch didn't hear the page. He had to make the dreaded call to the Marine base and tell them he missed the plane. Boy, were they mad! Mitch had to wait for the next available plane. Four hours later he was boarding for his destination.

When you first arrive on Parris Island you have to stand on a set of yellow footprints for processing. They make you put your personal items in a bag and tell you what they expect. Mitch missed this process because of the plane. Mitch was yelled at pretty badly and wasn't off to a good start. After they get processed they make them call home and they tell you exactly what to say. I could hear the sergeant in the background yelling, "This is Mitch, I have made it to Parris Island safely, do not call or try to redial this number, etc. etc" I could hear Mitch trying to listen to him yelling while he had to repeat every word. They do not let you talk or ask any questions and after they repeat what they are saying, the phone conversation is done. Then I wasn't allowed to talk to Mitch until after training. I thought to myself when hearing this, "Oh no! What did Mitch get himself into?"

Mitch was assigned to Platoon 2102, 2nd Battalion with Fox Company. The Marine motto is honor, courage and commitment. They believe, Once a Marine –Always a Marine. Semper Fidelis –Always faithful. They also like to say, you are not in the Marines, You are a Marine.

When Mitch started boot camp he said it was a lot of hard training. He had to learn the weapons inside and out. Mitch had to run several times a day. Even though it was hard he never wanted to give up. Mitch wanted to prove he could do it. There were about thirteen guys in the first three weeks of training that couldn't make it or had to start training all over. The women train on Parris Island too, but are separated from the guys.

Mitch made it through the basic training.

Once you pass everything that is required from the classroom training, shooting your gun, climbing a tower by rope, and bayonet combat training, they you are ready for the Crucible. Mitch actually started the Crucible on November 4th, his brother, Lucas' birthday. The Crucible is the hardest part that the new Marines will go through. It's a grueling three long days, fifty-seven hours, and they march fifty-three miles with full gear, eating only MRE's (meals ready to eat), and with only seven hours of sleep. Their backs are sore, along with their feet and they have a hard time at the end making it to the finish. With a lot of tears, screams, and determination they will make it to the finish line. Mitch told me that the drill sergeant would yell at him and say things about your "momma", family, friends and whatever they need to, to piss you off enough to make you so angry you finish. After the Crucible they have a breakfast fit for a King, because they deserve it after the hard work they put into it. After the big breakfast, it's onto the final days on their duty stations and a last inspection from the Battalion commander. I had found a poem that is wonderful on the Internet called, "Did You Know" by Janet Butterworth-Caldwell, if you get a chance to read it. That's how I felt about Mitch when he was going through the Crucible.

The first Sunday after the Crucible is called, "liberty" and they are allowed to call home and have free time. Mitch was talking to me on the phone and one of the drill instructors came up screaming at him. Mitch dropped the phone and stood at attention. The sergeant had instructed the guys to not spend their money on cell phones and had thought that Mitch had bought one. I was on a military Internet chat site and had said how worried I was. I thought I was just talking to other mom's who sons were on Parris Island. I had told this person on the chat site that Mitch was on the phone with me and I heard screaming then the phone dropped and went dead. I was worried that something was wrong because Mitch was using his friend's mom's cell phone and since it was liberty, it was Mitch's free time. Here it turned out it was one of the sergeant's wives I had told. She contacted her husband, and he called Mitch into his office to have him explain to him what was going on. After Mitch told him he had been using his friend's mom's cell phone, then the sergeant told Mitch to call me back and finish our conversation. He told Mitch to use his office to call me, and that he would pay for it. The sergeant apologized to Mitch and sent an email to me to apologize.

When we went to see Mitch graduate at Parris Island the first day is called, Family Day. We took a tour of the base. Temperatures were in the 70s in the daytime, and 50s and 60s in the evening. We had gotten the opportunity to see part of the tower, the gas chamber that they have to go through and surrounding areas of the Island. The drill instructor on the bus was telling us about how when he had to call home (when he was a new recruit at the Island), he forgot his phone number because the sergeant was yelling at him and he was so nervous. He said he was the only one left and looked around and the drill sergeant told him they would be there all night until he remembered his phone number. What he told us next had everyone on the bus laughing. He said since he couldn't remember the phone number, he dialed the operator. He said, this is so and so, I have reached Parris Island safely, do not call, and so on till the end. At the end the drill sergeant makes you tell the person on the other end of the phone you love them. At the end of the phone conversation this drill instructor (who was a recruit at the time) said to this operator, "I love you." He told us that the operator said, "Asshole!" He said this was his first phone call on Parris Island and his family was mad at him for not calling. He couldn't call them till after training, so they had no way of knowing if he made it there safely.

After our bus tour, they had the emblem ceremony to get their eagle, globe, and anchor pins. The eagle represents service for our country. The globe represents worldwide service. And, the anchor stands for naval (sea) traditions.

I looked for Mitch in the crowd of Marines and as I saw him, I started to cry because when they handed him his pin, you could see the tears of pride he had for all his hard work and dedication he put forth. He had accomplished a lot and it was well deserved. The Marines then put the pins on their hats. This shows them that they have completed their training and are now Marines. It's a time of great pride for the parents and the Marines. They do the flag ceremony along with their march, and then the drill instructor gets to yell at them one last time before releasing them. After the last, YES SIR! From the new Marines they are dismissed. The Marines all yell, "Ooh Rah!" Then everyone goes off with his or her families to spend the day. Mitch's brother, Lucas, John, and myself went to see this proud day. Mitch took us to a restaurant on base to eat, showed us around base at a military museum and we did a little shopping there.

The next day is the official graduation and Mitch's grandparents Gram and Pap Cresswell arrive. Each battalion had there own colors, and 2nd battalion was gold. John and Mitch's pap wore a gold Marine T-shirt, Lucas wore a green marine T-shirt with the gold letters of the word Marines and I wore a gold scarf around my neck. Mitch's gram just decided to go with what she had. She wasn't in the shopping mood.

We all took our seats and then the Marine band walked onto the platform, next the Marine mascot, which is a bulldog named, Iron Mike, then the Marines walk out. They said no one was ever buried at Parris Island except their first bulldog. The ceremonies were next with them announcing the honor graduates for the companies, platoon, marksmanship, awards, physical excellence and meritorious promotion (leadership). The Marines also receive a rifle exert pin, which they pin onto their uniforms. The military recognizes that it takes a lot of courage to join at wartime and they give each Marine a ribbon (bar).

When the band starts to play the Marine hymn, it is the end of the ceremonies. You can hear the pride with the Marines yelling, "Ooh-Rah!" And "Semper-fi!", Mitch is officially, allowed to be called Private. For some parents, this is the first time seeing their son's at graduation, and they can't wait to hug their son, whom they haven't seen for about three months. After graduation, our family met Mitch's three drill sergeants and his close friends. I took a lot of pictures to put in his album for when I got home.

When Mitch went to pick up his gear, a new recruit on duty was watching over the Marines gear. He said to Mitch, "Hi Sir", and gave a salute and stood at attention. I looked at Mitch and whispered, "He is saluting you." Mitch turned around to look for a sergeant and with none around he saluted the new recruit so he would release his at-attention stance. He said it seemed weird to him, but after graduation anyone who under ranks him, had to salute. Mitch just wasn't used to it yet.

Mitch only had seen his friend at Parris Island a few times. They were at different levels of training, and had only seen each other in passing while running. Mitch's friend from high school graduated two weeks before him. Now, after graduating it would be awhile before they'd see each other again. They had always done weight lifting together and went places while in school.

Mitch came home with us after the graduation ceremony for a few weeks in November, and we had our Thanksgiving meal before we drove him to Camp Geiger in North Carolina. Camp Geiger is called "The Marine Corp Air Station." He had to report on November 24th. Camp Geiger is near Jacksonville, N.C. Mitch would have more extensive training in combat skills and infantry, and also would have to attend classes as well as hand-to-hand combat training. We weren't able to go to see him graduate from this base, but he told us a lot of parents don't go to this one because they give them their graduation pin in private.

Mitch was at Camp Geiger when President Bush visited the troops for Thanksgiving in Baghdad. I put the Presidents speech in Mitchell's military album. Mitch spent two months at Camp Geiger and while there one day in December, the troops were hearing that Saddam was captured. Mitch called me right away to ask me if it was true, and I told him, "yes", that I was watching it on TV. He turned to his fellow

Marines in the barracks and repeated what I had said. I could hear them all cheering. It was a happy day for the military.

Mitch graduated from Camp Geiger in December of 2003, and came home for a few weeks over the Christmas holidays. While he was home he had to work as a recruiter's assistant. Mitch decided to take out a loan and bought his first car, which was a Honda. He now would experience what it would be like to have his first car payments.

In January of 2004, Mitch was headed off to Fort Leonardwood, Missouri. He continued there with more extensive training.

End Note (2008): After Mitch completed all of his training he was stationed at Twenty-Nine Palms, in California, where he served out the rest of his military requirements. Mitch is now out of the service.

The Foley's Christmas Letter
Of 2006

This is my first attempt at writing a Christmas newsletter so I hope you enjoy catching up on our family events as much as I have enjoyed writing it.

Another year has passed, and another Christmas is upon us, along with all of the hustle and bustle of the season. It's a time of celebration and for family to get together. It would be great to see all of you this year but if we don't get together, I hope this letter will catch you up on some of the things our family has been up for the past year.

Most of our family has gotten new jobs this year, except for John. John got recognition with his job as Trooper of the Year for his troop. This is not only for his barracks, but also extends to all of Troop G. Luke started as a prep cook at a local restaurant. Mitch started working for a construction company. I gave up doing my notary work after four years. I also officially gave up the secretarial job, to working in the medical records department. Landon's job is still being a kid but he has grown a lot and learning in leaps and bounds. He just turned four this year but he is already starting to be a master artist. Someday maybe he'll become the next Picasso.

We've all been busy with our hobbies. John loves to watch his sports. Yelling at the losers! Mitch has been tinkering with his big boy toys, cars and motorcycles and entering a car show or two. Luke has been doing some drawing and entered a poetry contest and we hope to hear back from them. Landon loves to swim and play outside. And, as far as me, I've been writing my memoirs, and still doing my scrapbooking after seven years.

I must add, I had a good year meeting a few famous people. I met Tawni O'Dell, as a speaker, along with her book signing. She got famous as an author as an Oprah Winphrey book club pick. She lives in State College now. I saw the Rascal Flatts country band perform at the Bryce Jordon Center (BYC) and met Jennifer Goodwin form WTAJ-TV10 news. Jennifer was one of the speakers at the Women's Club I belong to. I got to speak with her and our group learned a lot about broadcasting the news. I took Landon to see Dora the Explorer Show at the BYC.

Both, John and I took Landon to "Sand-Castle" in Pittsburgh in August, along with a boat ride down the Three Rivers. Later in October, we took Landon to "Splash Lagoon" in Erie, PA to an indoor water park. I'm happy to report he had loads of fun at both places. Landon loves splashing in the water. Maybe, he'll become an Olympic swimmer someday.

John and I took a vacation this year to Washington, DC. Unfortunately, we went at the hottest time of the year in August. We drank a ton of water, or at least it felt like it. It was a scorcher. I took a lot of photos, and we saw the White House, Arlington Cemetery where JFK's torch burns, and the changing of the guard. We took in a lot of sites including some of the Washington, DC area in town, the monuments, and went into some of the museums. One of my favorite must-have photos was of Archie and Edith Bunker chairs from "All in the Family" TV show. Another photo opportunity was Dorothy's red shoes from the "Wizard of Oz".

In October, John and I celebrated our thirteen-year anniversary. At Thanksgiving the family decided to all go out to eat at a local restaurant this year. Eating in or out, we still have a lot to be thankful for even though this year has brought a few unpleasant events. Mitch's car was broken into. Yes, the one he likes to enter in car shows. Luke has had some setbacks, and, Luke and Mitch's Gram and Pap (on their dad's side) both died this year. Luke and Mitch both had to deal with that loss. But, we are thankful our family is healthy.

We will be spending Christmas at home with our family cooking turkey with all the fixings. We'll turn the Christmas tree lights on, and in the background Christmas music will be playing while we open our presents. The real joy will be seeing Landon's face light up when he sees his presents under the tree. We hope to have a white Christmas day. Notice I said, day. Snowflakes and snowmen are nice to have on Christmas day, and then I'd be happy with sunshine.

Wishing your family well, we hope all your wishes come true and you have a joyous Christmas. Ring in the New Year of 2007 with the traditional sauerkraut for good luck throughout the New Year, and don't forget the mashed potatoes, along with some new resolutions.

Love,

Barb and John

Blue Spruce in Our Backyard

If Walls Could Talk

If walls could talk, what would your walls say? Did you have a wedding gathering in your house? A Christmas where laughter was all around you? Was there a death in the family?

What would our walls say about the kitchen? It would say; family, love, romance, home cooking, laughter, tears and a broken glass or two. It used to be our family would all gather at my parent's house for Christmas dinner. A Christmas dinner at my parents consisted of what I'd call lunch which is at 11:30 am. Now, at my house our Christmas meal is around 2 p.m. This works out better for our family as a lunch/dinner. Eat one time and you're full the rest of the day. My parents now come to our house to eat this meal. A lot of home-cooked meals were made in our kitchen. Some were delicious, some not so delicious, and some were new recipes. I remember making a dish that had cabbage, raisins, some type of glaze and it was awful. We haven't had that since. Then there are the most wonderful dishes like slow cooked roast beef, mashed potatoes, gravy, corn and many others.

The kitchen has also seen wonderful times such as rocking a newborn, heating up bottles, and even a little kiss between my husband and me. The kitchen is where homework was done with all its frustrations. Then there were the happy report cards coming home with good grades and some not so good. Some of my collections are displayed in the kitchen. I have a skunk collection. Skunks fill the room everywhere from my display case to salt and peppershakers to photos of skunks on the wall. Mostly Pepe Le-Pew. Who could resist the romantic Pepe trying to court a cat named Penelope who he thinks is a skunk? Recently, I started to collect folk-art teapots.

Well, what would the living room say? Maybe the living room would give more clues into our life. For instance, another collection waits in this room. The living room has the carousel horse collection in a display case to photos of carousels on the wall. We've cried and laughed in this room watching all our favorite television shows anywhere from great movies, to sitcoms, to comedy, to love stories, to war movies. We laughed with Jerry Seinfield, All in The Family, and Two and a Half Men. We cried when Princess Diana died. We were glued to the TV with the tragedy on September 11, 2001 when the twin towers went down. And, we also watched news shows like Nancy Grace, Bill O'Reiley and Anderson Cooper. Then there were shows like Lost and trying to figure out the island, Prison Break, Survivor and others. My husband also yelled at the TV when his favorite sport teams were losing.

The living room has been a place where we visited with family and friends, watched our babies take naps, witnessed fights between brothers, hanging Christmas lights and opening presents. Landon celebrated his birthdays in this room and even broke a piñata for Easter, instead of the traditional Easter basket. Landon learned how to walk in this room and we've read to him before bedtime. Landon has watched Ghostbusters over and over and has changed his name to Dr. Peter Venkman, a character from the movie who is played by Bill Murray. Landon loves to sing the Ghostbuster theme song, "There's something strange in the neighborhood and it don't look good, who are you going to call? Ghost Busters!" The living room would definitely say give Landon some chocolate milk before bedtime. While drinking his chocolate milk you must turn the TV on to Sponge Bob Square Pants before going to bed.

Continuing the tour of the house and the talking walls we go down the stairs where the hallway is full of family photos. John calls this hallway; "the hall of fam", as in the hall of fame. Then we're off to the family room. This room has John's collections of his model state police cars and his golf balls with logos. John collects golf balls from places we visit while on vacation. Since we don't go on a lot of vacations this one is still not full. But, if you look on the other wall, you will find Landon's Pez collection. The Pez case holds ninety-two Pez and it is totally full with some having to lie on the top of the case. You will also find all of

64

Landon's toys from stuffed animals, to trucks and cars, to Spiderman and Ghostbusters. Landon loves to play yard sale but if you'd go to one of his yard sales everything is free. But we're only pretending. I believe this is where Landon's imaginary friend started. One day he was playing and said he was playing with Dee Dee Dirt. Then it became a joke of who is Dee Dee Dirt? Landon would say; "I don't know" and he would tell us he's just pretend. Dee Dee Dirt shows up once in awhile and from time to time. He's a good imaginary friend just coming and going to say hello and good-bye while passing through. Dee Dee Dirt however goes on a lot of vacations.

Moving along, the gym room has had plenty of sweat. If walls could talk they would be asking; "Are you going to work out today?" It would be a battle to see if the living room couch would win or the treadmill. Sometimes the couch would win and other times the treadmill or weights would win. Once in awhile an exercise video of Jane Fonda or Leslie Sansone would be thrown into the mix. It would be nice if this room were used more often.

If you come visit me, and you have spent the day going from room to room, what would the bedroom tell you? One thing the bedroom would tell you is to never go to bed angry. Work things out before going to sleep. Always give each other a goodnight kiss. And, if we have our grandson with us, we sing nursery rhymes. The childhood nursery rhyme songs started with Landon and now each of us has to sing a few songs before going to sleep. There's Itsy Bitsy Spider, Jack and Jill, Humpty Dumpty, Old Mother Hubbard, Three Blind Mice, Hickory Dickory Dock and Landons all time favorite the Heat Miser from a Christmas Show. We used to sing Twinkle Twinkle Little Star, but Landon says it's too babyish now so it's off limits. This is when Landon was four. Landon's other favorite song is; "Sam Sam the Butcher Man, washed his face in a frying pan, combed his hair with a wagon wheel, and died with a toothpick in his heel". The key to this song is to sing it with a hillbilly accent.

I hope you enjoyed your tour of our house with "If walls could talk", till next time ...

Passing Out
(My Dad)

My dad passed out in September of 2006. My mom got frightened and wanted to take him to the hospital but he wouldn't go. "Old school" thinking tells him not to ask for help. So he got up after about 15 minutes and went about his business. A few days later he got wobbly. His legs didn't want to move. He knew he was going to fall and aimed for the chair. This time he got it right on. Dad didn't pass out this time, a good sign.

My mom finally talked dad into going to the doctor in November. The doctor told my dad that his heart was okay and no sign of an oncoming stroke. They told him it could be his kidneys or some other problems. The doctor said; "It looks like your insides are all messed up." Whatever that means. The doctor told him they would have to do more tests, but they would have to set up an appointment for him right after Christmas. The doctor also told my dad that he is good to go home and will see him in a month.

Christmas comes around the corner. I've invited my parents to eat with us for dinner. I usually have my dinner around two in the afternoon. This time I had my dinner at noon since my parents like to eat early. It's strange having dinner so early, but sort of nice in a way knowing I will have the remainder of the day to rest.

Landon was staying with us and got up around eight in the morning and opened his presents. He is four years old. What a great age to watch a child be excited about all his gifts. Everyone starts to arrive between ten and eleven. My son, Mitch, drove to Huntingdon to pick up his wife, Ebony, and stepson, Malik. Ebony brought Malik's gifts along with her since he spent the morning with his dad and other grandparents. I took pictures of Landon and Malik while checking on the meal. Melissa (Landon's mom) arrived.

I glanced up at the clock. It's 12 noon and my meal is ready. My parents are never late. Where are my parents? I start to worry right away, but know they would have called if they weren't coming. I start to think awful thoughts. What if they got in a wreck? What if something happened to dad? What if something happened to my mom? She's always at the doctors too, because her blood count is low.

Finally, they arrive. It's about 12:15. The table is full. There are nine people total for our dinner. The meal is ready and we do the last details. I always wait until the last minute to mash the potatoes. Dad looks weak. He has a hard time coming up the steps but makes it to the kitchen. He sits down with the rest of us. We know there's something wrong, but are not sure what. My mom tells us she had to drive part way. This is major for my dad.

Everyone is talking small talk and sitting around reminiscing about the past. Mitch makes a comment to my dad to try and make him laugh. He musters a smile but it's forced. He seems lethargic. My dad normally is a big eater. This meal, though, he only eats a bite or two of turkey and very little of the mashed potatoes. Normally, my parents won't drink anything at a meal but my dad asks for a soda. This was just how they were brought up. They never were allowed to have a drink at their meals until they were done eating. My dad skips the pies. Something is seriously wrong. My dad loves to eat and especially loves sweets, as do I.

My mom says they better head back home since my dad isn't feeling well. Dad couldn't get out of the chair. I knew he was having trouble and didn't want to admit he couldn't stand up. I whisper to my husband that dad can't get up which is why he's sitting there while my mom is telling him she wants to go. When mom has to drive she doesn't want to linger since it's an hour drive home. John, my husband, walks over to my dad and tells him; "Let me give you a hand." Dad stands. John says he will help him to the car and we insist he can't drive. For once he agrees. Everyone looks at each other with worry. We try and get him to go to the hospital but he won't hear of it. John and I offer to take them home. John would drive my dad's car and I would follow to bring him back home. They both decline the offer. My mom tells us my dad has a doctor's appointment in about two weeks. This seems way too long to wait.

A week went by, and I got a call from my mom saying my dad fell again. He got wobbly and his legs wouldn't move. Dad tried to get to his chair and couldn't. "He didn't pass out this time", my mom told me, but she did have to call my brother to help get him up. My dad is a big man. My mom was going to call the ambulance but my dad wouldn't let her. The moment passed. My brother helped my dad to bed and in the morning he seemed fine again.

Later that day my mom got my dad to agree to go to the VA hospital in Altoona to get checked. When they got there they told him since he didn't have an appointment he'd have to go to the Altoona hospital. Unbelievably, my dad agreed to go. They took some blood work and told him to wear a heart monitor for the night. The doctors told him they wanted him to stay the night because whatever was wrong could be life threatening. They told him it looks like his insides are all messed up. My dad, being dad, told the doctors there was no way he can stay the night. It's Monday, and he is worried about getting to the bank to make a car payment. He told them no and went home with the heart monitor on. He got a doctor appointment to go back to the VA hospital in a few days.

Wednesday came and as agreed my dad got ready to be admitted to the VA hospital. They told him they want to keep him for three to four days. My mom got dad admitted and she returned home. Mom said she needed to go to work the next day. A lot of her medical bills aren't covered under their plan and since she has to go to the doctors every three weeks or so herself, she didn't want to call off of work. My parents are so bull-headed. My husband and I have been trying to get my dad and mom to apply for a lift chair for my dad, but they just don't like to take any help from anyone.

John and I planned on seeing my dad on Friday, since mom said it looked like he wouldn't get out of the hospital till Sunday. I told my mom to call me when she got off work and we'd meet her up there. Around two in the afternoon, my mom called to say my dad was getting released, and we didn't need to run up to Altoona. Mom told us she has been sick all day, throwing up and having diarrhea. John and I insisted we'd go to the hospital to pick up my dad and take him home.

We arrived at the VA hospital around 4 pm. When we went into the room and I looked at my dad he looked like he aged at least ten years, if not more, in the last three months. He lost over forty pounds, his hair seemed to turn pure gray, and for the first time he actually looked like a grandfather to me instead of my dad. My dad is usually a person on the go, doing things, and never seemed old to me until this day.

I asked dad; "What did they find out?" He told me he has diabetes and was dehydrated. The doctors told him he didn't have any mini-stokes, or a heart attack, and everything else seemed normal, but they told him he was lucky that nothing worse had happened to him. The doctors said it is life threatening and to take it seriously. Dad isn't allowed to have sweets anymore. No soda, candy, pies and ice cream. No junk food. This is going to be extremely hard for him. The doctor asked dad; "Why didn't you stay when we wanted you to?" And, my dad replied, "Just bull-headed, I guess."

Dad has a lot of doctor appointments lined up. They have to play around with the medicine to get it just right for him. It just goes to show you, one day you're fine and the next day your life could be in jeopardy. I think my dad was afraid of what the doctors would tell him. I think he thought it was going to be devastating news. Although, diabetes is a bad disease, it could have been worse. This has taught me a lesson to go to the doctor when something is wrong instead of letting it get worse. Dad could have been starting to feel better a month or two ago. I have to admit, I am a lot like my dad when it comes to going to the doctor when I think I could receive bad news. Never assume.

69

It's unbelievable that in just a few short months my dad went from looking young for his age to looking like his age. My parents have both always looked at least 20 years younger than their real age. They're both 76 years old. It's all so sad. When we got to their house he told my mom what all the doctor said, and then he repeated himself a few times as if he were talking to himself and trying to let it sink in. "Yeah, I have diabetes…I have diabetes…"

End Note: I am happy to report that now two years later (2008), my dad is looking like his younger self once again.

(See a photo of my mom and dad in the photo section.)

Kids
(What the heck are they up to now?)

I was visiting my sister where she lived on Fairground road in Huntingdon, and our children were playing outside. It was a cold day, and the snow was drifting off to just a few flurries. My son, Lucas, and my sister's son, Roger, were making a snowman. They wanted to try and make the biggest one anyone had ever seen. Lucas was around twelve years old, and Roger, was around eight years old. They were pushing the snowball back and forth in rows as to get the ball bigger and bigger. Janet's house has a big hill in the back yard where the boys were playing.

My sister and I were sitting inside just chatting over cups of coffee. Lucas and Roger could no longer push the snowball because it was getting so big. They really weren't thinking about the hill that they were on until the ball started to roll down. By this time the snowball was so big that they were afraid if they let the ball just roll, it would keep getting bigger, and hit one of the cars sitting by the house. So, Lucas got this bright idea to try and stop it while it was picking up speed coming down the hill.

All of a sudden my sister and I heard this big THUMP! We ran outside to see what was going on, and Lucas was pinned up against the house with the big snowball in front of him, and he couldn't move. It took my sister, Roger, and myself, to help get this thing off of him. When we finally got it off Lucas, the siding on the house looked like Wile E. Coyote in the cartoon with Lucas' imprint of his body. He wasn't hurt, just a little sore, bruised and scared. We all laughed after we knew he was okay.

My sister and I have learned over the years that when these two get together they can get into a pickle, and be very inventive. Roger hated to mow grass when he reached about ten years old, but this was one of his chores. He got to brainstorming and come up with a clever way to keep the boredom at bay while cutting grass. Roger's favorite nascar driver was Dale Earnhart, the number three car. This was Dale senior, as Dale Jr. hadn't driven in the races yet at the time. Roger went to the shed and got some paint and a brush, and started his masterpiece. He created the ultimate lawn mower. The Dale Earnhart supper mower! That mower was the spitting image of Dale's car. While his lawn mower was in working condition he didn't complain about mowing grass. When the Dale Earnhart mower broke down, then it had to be worked on in the cockpit of the garage till it was fixed. There was no other acceptable mower to mow the lawn with.

It doesn't stop there. Kids can get themselves in trouble in other ways. My younger son, Mitch, who was in first grade, at the time, could never sit still. The teacher yelled at him for fidgeting, and Mitch stood up by his desk, and started to wiggle his butt back and forth, and said, "I don't have to listen to you, cause you're not my mom." Well, it wouldn't have been so bad if that were all there was to it, but I got a call from the teacher. She told me I'd have to sit Mitch down and talk to him about his disruptive behavior. I asked her if that was the first time he'd ever done this, and she said, "Yes, but then the whole class got up to do the same thing." She continued, "Have you ever seen a whole class get up off their seats, wiggle their butts back and forth, and say they don't have to listen to me because I'm not their mom?"

I said, "No, I haven't." I was trying not to burst into laughter while she was on the phone. I did, however, explain to Mitch while keeping a straight face why this behavior was unacceptable.

Years later, my husband, John, was watching Mitch while I went somewhere with a friend of mine. I arrived home to find ALL of the neighborhood leaves in my yard. Mitch was around ten years old now, he had gotten together with one of his friends, and they decided to take a wheel barrel and go around asking all the neighbors if they could have their leaves. Of course, they didn't mind. Why would they? The two boys were raking their yards, it was free, and they even had gotten free leaf removal. What more could you ask for? Except if you were me. I had to wonder, what the heck was I going to do with all those leaves? This wasn't just a couple of people either. It was around twenty or more homes they cleaned the leaves from. The one good thing that came out of it, I guess, was that the leaf collector only had to stop at our house.

I started to wonder if there was something in our family's genes. Maybe, it was handed down from generation to generation. Years passed, and Mitch, twenty years old, had to have me pick him up from a friend's house. My grandson, Landon, two and a half years old, had his moment to shine. I said to Landon, "Let's go pick up Mitch." Landon said, "Don't wanna pick up Mitch." I looked at him and asked him, "Why?" Landon said with a serious look on his face, "He's too heavy." I "busted up" laughing, and tried to explain to Landon that's not what I meant. Another time when Landon was around three, I asked him how he got so smart. He replied, "From eating smarties." (Smarties are a sweet tart candy.) There's nothing like seeing life through the eyes of a child to make you think, and keep life interesting. I am glad we have those moments. After all, laughter is the best medicine.

(See a photo of the boys in the photo section.)

Anorexia Nervosa

About twenty years ago my sister was severely over weight. She probably weighed around 290 lbs. Her husband kept nagging her about her weight whether for cosmetic reasons or health reasons, I don't know. I believe at the time it was more because he felt embarrassed by her. Somewhere along the line she got it in her head that she was going to lose weight at all cost. This idea may have cost her…her life.

When I first saw Janet when she put her summer clothes on, I was taken aback. Instead of the 110 pounds she was telling people she was, which is still too much weight loss for someone at 5'5", she had gone down to about 90 Lbs. She literally looked like you could eat a bowl of cereal out of her chest. Her chest had sunken in and all you could see was a round hole and her ribs. She was withering away.

Janet was diagnosed with Anorexia Nervosa. Anorexia is an illness where you just stop eating and exercise excessively. It occurs mostly in teenage girls, but boys can also become victim of it. Janet's started as an adult. People with anorexia become obsessed with being thin, and believe they are fat even though they are not. They also may exercise compulsively which is called, Anorexia Athletica. Janet woke up early in the mornings to exercise with Richard Simmons, Joanie Greggins or Gilad; all TV exercise fitness guru's. Sometimes two, three and even four times a day. She would exercise about an hour each session. She got it in her head that in order to lose weight faster; she would just stop eating except maybe once a day. Eventually, she lost the excessive weight, but kept losing. In her mind she was just as fat at 90 lbs as she was at 290 lbs.

Janet said she'd only eat between 450 to 500 calories a day. Not enough food to sustain anyone. The nutritionist had Janet's household remove all mirrors and the weight scales. They removed the mirrors because they didn't want her to see if she was gaining anything. This would have been a set back in Janet's mind. She also wasn't allowed to weigh herself. If she had noticed herself gaining weight, she would have stopped eating.

I recently asked Janet about how someone who has Anorexia thinks. How can you not eat food? I can't imagine not eating. It's just not in my vocabulary. Janet said; "If I would have not been scared, I would have made myself throw up." She said she could never bring herself to do it. She just stopped eating. The difference between Anorexia and Bulimia is that anorexics starve themselves and don't eat much or at all. Bulimics eat huge amounts of food, but then throw up after eating. Sometimes they take laxatives or water pills to keep from gaining. Anorexics will even sometimes make huge amounts of food for their family and then eat none of it or small portions. In Janet's case she barely ate at all and mostly stuck with salads or a piece of toast and coffee. This is what she ate for the whole day.

I then asked Janet; "Weren't you hungry?" She said, "Yes at times but I felt like I could control my hunger pains." Janet said, "I would just work through the hunger, it was better than being fat."

Janet said one of the things that someone is thinking when he or she has Anorexia is that the weight is the only thing the person can control. It makes sense, since at the time she was having marital problems and some other issues. Janet couldn't control what the people around her were doing, but she could take control of her weight.

She was using losing weight to deal with the emotional problems she was having. Janet thought by losing the weight she could fix the problems in her marriage.

Janet's husband, her mother-in-law, along with our family had to convince her to seek medical attention. She didn't think there was anything wrong. They had gotten a nutritionist who would make a house call and teach Janet how to eat so she could put some weight back on and keep the weight off. Janet was terrified of putting on weight. I think she would have rather died than to put that weight back on. The nutritionist, along with the doctors didn't think she would make it, and told us privately so Janet wouldn't hear. Although, I do remember them eventually having to tell my sister that she will die if she didn't listen. They also threatened her that if she didn't start putting on weight then they would commit her to a hospital. I think Janet was more terrified of that. She didn't want to go to an inpatient care hospital for an eating disorder. She knew she'd have to stay there awhile before being released. Janet didn't want to be away from her husband and children.

The doctors and nutritionist did get Janet's weight back up to a reasonable weight. She maintains her weight around 120 pounds now, and has, ever since the family intervened. Some people do need to be hospitalized but Janet refused to go so they got someone to come to her. She did, however, get counseling for both nutrition and her emotional problems. Most people need both as it starts in most cases by trying to control some part of your life. Janet also suffered from low self-esteem and felt worthless.

To this day she still has to tell herself to eat. She usually eats a piece of toast with several cups of coffee in the morning and then when her husband wants dinner, she eats a small portion of that. Now and then, she will have some chips or candy, but it is rare.

End Note: *Anorexia is life threatening which can cause death from starvation. If you think someone you know is suffering from an eating disorder, please seek medical advice on how to get him or her help. One percent of teen girls (some cases even boys) in the U.S. develops Anorexia Nervosa (that means about one out of every one hundred are starving themselves), and up to 10% of those die as a result. (Statistics found on the Internet.)*

Here are some warning signs of Anorexia
Deliberate starvation with weight loss
Fear of gaining weight
Refusal to eat
Denial of hunger
Absent or irregular periods
Constant exercising
Sensitivity to cold temperatures
Loss of scalp hair
Someone who says they are fat even when they are really too thin

---

(See a photo of Janet when she was young in the photo section.)

Easter 2008

The Easter bunny was to arrive on Sunday, March 23rd. A bit early this year and according to people who predict these things, we will not see another early Easter like this in our lifetime. Only people who are now at least 95 years old has ever seen it this early. Easter is always the first Sunday after the first full moon after the Spring Equinox (which is March 21).

Here are a few facts:

1) The next time Easter will be this early (March 23) will be the year 2228 (220 years from now).

2) The next time it will be a day earlier, March 22, will be in the year 2285 (277 years from now).

3) The last time it was on March 22 was 1818.

4) Next year Easter will come even later — April 12.

5) Easter can never occur before March 22 or later than April 25.

Landon, our grandson, doesn't eat much candy. His favorite candy is a "Kit Kat" bar. He'll eat a piece, here and there, but it's not something he has to have. I will give you an example, but we must rewind a bit to about a week earlier. We were at Wal-Mart to pick up some pictures I had developed. Working our way out of the store to the check out counter, we had to go past the Easter candy. Well, maybe we didn't have to, but I wanted to. Unfortunately, this is one of my downfalls. Anyway, I asked Landon if he wanted some candy. He said, "No." I waited a little bit, then asked him again; "Landon, are you sure you don't want some candy?" He said; "No! I told you I don't want any candy." Some guy in the store turned around and said; "You better get him checked out for a fever." He's right, that most kids wouldn't turn down the opportunity to get some candy. But, Landon really doesn't care for it much. He'd rather have toys.

Although this Easter there was something else even bigger on his mind; he wanted a suit. Yes, that's right, a five-year old boy wanting a suit! Can you imagine? He had the specifics down, a black suit with vest, jacket and a red bow tie. No other tie would do, it had to be a red bow tie. We had already put our order in to the Easter bunny of things to get for Landon, so I called his parents to let them know what Landon wanted. Landon wanted to look like Pap. Pap gets dressed up for court. Not sure where the idea of the red bow tie came from, since Pap doesn't wear bow ties.

Landon woke up on Easter day to a big sand bucket of candy, since it seem to be more appropriate than a basket. The Easter Bunny had seen reason with this one. John, Landon and I will be going on vacation to Myrtle Beach this summer and a sand bucket and shovel was the way to go. Landon also got a game called, "3D Labyrinth." He loves this game. The board moves back and forth to try and get through a maze. He also got a 100-piece puzzle, which he seemed to breeze through, a tea set that he's been wanting, and some finger puppets, so he could put on a puppet show.

The day for Landon started out really well, playing a game or two with Pap, and a tea party with Gram, Shrek, Donkey, Puss-n-Boots and a stuffed bunny he had gotten from the Easter bunny. Some of us had to share a cup since we only had four cups. Shrek being green got the green tea cup and saucer, Donkey and Gram got yellow, Landon and the bunny had a blue cup, and the pink, which no animals wanted, went to Puss-n-Boots.

Since the Easter Bunny arrived the day before at his other Pap's house (he calls this pap, "Old Pap") and his Dad's place, he only had two more places to go. Landon knew that the Easter Bunny had also visited where his mom and other grandmother lives. He calls his other grandma, "The Gram with the black truck." So, he figured the suit had to be there. *(Landon calls us just "Gram" and "Pap". I think it's because he lives with us.)*

Landon got ready to go with his mom and Gram with the black truck. They would be coming back later since we made reservations to "The Gardens" restaurant for John, Landon and myself.

When he came home, he had on his suit. He had a black suit with the vest and pants, white shirt and a tie. He didn't get the jacket but I think he was okay with that. The first thing Landon said was; "Look what the Easter bunny brought me! A suit!" but with disappointment on his face continued; "It has a regular tie, and I wanted a red bow tie." Landon set the tone for our meal because he was wearing his suit. John got his suit on and I wore dressy clothes. After we were all ready to go to the restaurant, Landon looked at Pap and said; "Pap, you look almost as good as me".

End Note: A few days later, we went searching for the red bow tie. After going to a lot of different stores, we finally found a black bow tie at Sears. We bought this one, but are still on the search for the red bow tie. Bow ties are hard to find now a days.

Easter (2008)

Bruised

Note: *(The name, "Blake" is a fictitious name. Everything else in the story is true.)*

I always liked to think that all people were good and would never harm you. It was July 1978 and I was having open-heart surgery for a hole in my heart. The doctor said it was the size of a half dollar, and if I didn't have it done I would be unable to have children, or I'd die having them. In 1978 heart surgery was still considered very risky. My parents asked my boyfriend whom I had been dating for about a year, to ride along to Cleveland Clinic in Ohio to see me. He decided to go camping with his friends instead.

Ginger, a brown and white border collie seen right through the evil that was lurking. Ginger was a mellow dog, never growled at anyone and would greet visitors. She even loved cats and left them sleep on top of her in the winter to help her stay warm. My mom would never allow animals in the house, so she'd sleep outside on the porch or her dog box. I would sit on the porch and swing with her for hours in the summertime. The only person Ginger ever nip at the heels of was my boyfriend, "Blake."

I should have seen the signs. I was seventeen years old, and naïve. We got married a few years later. We bought a trailer and put it on his dad's piece of ground. Blake's dad was abusive to his mother for years. Another sign I overlooked. A few years later after our marriage, Blake started becoming extremely jealous. He didn't want me to be around my friends or talk to my family for any length of time.

It was almost like scene from a movie the first time Blake hit me. It was bitter cold, raining, and shadows from the trees were swaying back and forth. I should have read the signs. I was young and didn't know any better. There were other things like being a daddy's boy, the possessiveness of not wanting me to be out of his sight. He whined like a baby when I wanted to visit my family and friends. If I would even say "hello" to another guy, I'd be hit. Eventually, you learn not to say anything to anyone. Blake started listening to all my phone conversations. Even though I never gave him any reason to disbelieve me, he found a reason why he should. When I had a job he would sit in the bushes across from where I worked with a pair of binoculars to see if I'd talk to anyone. If I did, I knew about it when I got home.

One time, Blake, hid in the trunk of my car to see where I'd go. I felt this eerie presence around me. When I got out of the car, I noticed the trunk ajar a tiny bit. I hurried up and went to slam the trunk shut. I figured who ever it was, I was going to drive to the police station and let him out there. I didn't know it was Blake. As soon as I went to slam the trunk shut, he pushed it open with his hands. Scared me to death! Another time he hid in the back seat of my car and I didn't know it. I was driving when he popped up behind my seat. A near heart attack!

I soon would have two children within three years. My middle child was stillborn. I had a rough time getting over that, and didn't want to talk to anyone afterwards for about two years. So, it was easy not talking to anyone. I took care of my older son and kept quiet for the most part. A few years later, my younger son arrived and I was overjoyed. My youngest son had some health problems in the beginning, but they were soon overcome.

After the years passed Blake had me mentally and physically beat. He made me feel worthless. He told me no one would ever want someone with two children. Every time he'd hit me, he'd cry, say how sorry he was and it would never happen again. I wanted to believe him. Things would be okay for about two weeks and then the cycle started all over again. It wasn't all bad, all the time, there were the in between times. We'd take our sons to the parks, go swimming, watch the fireworks and do little things here and there.

Things seemed to be getting worse for each passing year. Blake wanted to buy a house and I think that was partly because in his mind it was a way to keep me there. We found a home and the bank approved the loan. The inspections were done and the house was ready to move into. We just had to wait three days and it would be finalized.

I started to get a sick feeling of being trapped, and stuck like a prisoner in my own home. Around the time the papers were getting ready to go through, this song called, "Fast Car" by Tracy Chapman came out. I listened to that song over and over. I started to believe in the one verse. It was, "I have to leave today or live and die this way." When I got in my car to go somewhere, I thought about keeping on driving. I could also hear the train near my house, and numerous times I thought about hoping on the train with my two children and taking off. How could we survive? My youngest child was in diapers and I had no money. I went to the assistance office for help and was in a catch twenty-two. They told me that I needed a place of my own to get help, and I needed money to get my own place. So, things went on as there were.

Meantime, I didn't take the song, "Fast Car" lightly. That song never left my mind and you could say it saved my children's and my life, as corny as that may sound. I decided if I didn't leave I would live and die this way. I had to make a plan. I knew if I went through with the loan for the house, I'd be there forever. My name would be on the loan, so I called up the loan company and told them to take my name off the loan. They asked me, "Why? It will be final in only a few days." I told them briefly and begged them not to say a word to Blake until the next week. I started packing and hid our clothes in places that wouldn't seem obvious. I planned on a Saturday to leave when Blake would be at work. I called a friend to help me move. I found a small apartment and rented it with the money I was saving when I could without it being noticed.

We got moved in but I only took our clothes because I didn't want any retaliation from Blake. I found out that when Blake got home, he was in a rage. He started breaking things up. I left a note telling him we had left him. It may seem like a cowards way to tell someone, but when you fear for your life and the lives of your children, then you got to do what you got to do. I always parked my car about two blocks away from where I was renting so he wouldn't find me. I figured the more time that would go by, the better.

I know a lot of people wonder why someone stays with someone that is abusive. Some people even think anyone who stays deserves what they got. It must not be too bad or you'd leave. Right? Wrong! It's not that easy. There are money issues, the children, and there's always the hope that the person you married would change as promised. But, I will tell you the biggest reason women stay in their abusive relationships, including me. FEAR! I feared for my life and the lives of my children. I believed him when he told me he'd kill me, and my children. I know because he would rig knives up to the window in case I would try to get out or in; whichever way he wanted it at the time. He threatened to take away the most important people in my life…my children.

After he found out where I lived, he broke my door down and I got evicted. Yes, they evicted my children and I because of him. I had a hard time renting because anyone who knew him didn't want to rent to me. I even had one lady that said anyone who knew Blake she wouldn't rent to and hung up on me. I finally found a place close to the next county that someone would rent out to us. It took several years and a lot of fines and Protection from Abuse Orders (PFAs) for him to finally start to leave me alone. I couldn't date anyone for a few years, because anyone I tried to date, he would destroy those relationships.

When I would see people who I knew, and I would talk to them, they would look at me like the cat just gave me back my tongue. Some people said, "Wow! I didn't even know you could talk." I told them, "When you get hit for even saying "Hi" to someone, you learn to not talk at all. As much as you believe you love someone who abuses you, your love can turn to hate with the same intensity.

I went for child support, but every time I'd try to get some money to feed and cloth the children, Blake would quit his job. I had to fight tooth and nail to even get domestic relations to have him pay ten dollars every two weeks. That didn't even cover one child's lunch ticket. When Blake went in to get that lowered, that was it. I waited till Blake left the room and asked the domestic relations coordinator at the time, "You aren't going to make him pay for anything are you?" His response was, "Well, Blake is just too difficult to handle". I told them right then, I will never come back again. I was losing money every time they had a hearing to get basically nothing down to even more of a big fat, Zero! I tried to use the system the right way to get child support, but no one knew what I was up against. No one wanted to deal with Blake because they thought that if they gave me what I wanted (which was child support), or anyone who helped me thought, that Blake would find them and destroy their property. There were too many people afraid to deal with him.

I always used to think that someday my ex would get what's coming to him, and he'd have to go through the same hell he put my children and me through. Over the years my ex has gotten away with so much. I started to feel like some people just get away with stuff and he will never be punished for what he has put my children and me through. But, I finally realized I am not the one to judge him. God will do that. I have come not to hate Blake, and will not waste my time and energy doing so. I had survived and left an abuser and made it. I may never forgive him, but will tolerate him for my children and grandchildren's sake.

Soon Blake would find out that someone would want to marry me with two children. After seven years of being on my own and raising my children myself, I got married to a man who treats me with respect and dignity. John is the complete opposite of my ex and thank God for that. We have been married now for fifteen years. I believe God has heard the cries of my children and me and has given me peace and a good life now. Sometimes when you go through hell, you come out of it a stronger person.

I have grown over the years. I used to be timid, shy, and afraid to turn my back because someone maybe stalking me. But now I am more mature, and the lies Blake told me are not true, and I know that now.

I tell this story because I hope that someday the women (or some men) who are abused will not believe the lies these people tell you and get out at the first sign of abuse. I had noticed that when I was dating in those few years, if someone abuses their mother or treats her with disrespect, in most cases, that's how they will treat you. If someone wants to keep you isolated from family and friends, and won't let you speak your mind, then, don't walk, RUN! And, keep running until you find someone who will let you be yourself.

Freedom always comes at a price and mine did to. I have the scars to show for it, but it was a decision I would never regret.

Tricks & Pranks

The first eleven years of my life I grew up at Raystown until the government came along and bought everyone's homes to start building Lake Raystown. I have an older brother, Richard, my sister, Janet, and then I'm the youngest. You would think that the older children usually pick on the youngest. But, in my case, it's just the opposite.

Raystown was fun for me as a kid growing up. We lived between two neighbors. Our house sat down in a hollow and the neighbors were each up on a hill on opposite sides of us. Both neighbors had girls, and my sister and I always played with them.

Janet always ran around with Beverly and I ran around with Becky, but for some unknown reason one day we switched whom we were going to play with. All of us were fighting that day but no one knows why. Beverly and I saw Janet and Becky getting onto Becky's motorcycle. Well, if you could call it a motorcycle. It was very small and kiddish but it was still real and took gas to run it. We were all name calling at each other and making faces back and forth. Becky and Janet were so involved in what Beverly and I were saying and doing that they ran smack into a tree. I saw Janet jump off the back really quickly. They were so mad at us that you could have seen smoke coming out of their ears. I think they were madder at us for laughing at them than they were for actually wrecking the motorcycle. We were laughing so hard that tears were streaming down our cheeks.

That wasn't the only time my sister ran into something. My mom needed to go into town and we had to go with her. We were walking down the street past McCrory's and Murphy's, which were called "five and dime" stores. I saw my sister getting close to one of the parking meters on the street. Well, being that I liked to pull pranks on her, I told her to look up at a bird that was flying over her head. And, suddenly you heard, SMACK!

She walked right into the meter. Oh Yeah! I laughed but who wouldn't when you're kids trying to outdo each other.

That wasn't the end of things that we pulled on each other. One time when I was playing with Becky, we hid Beverly and Janet's snow disks (also known as pan sleds) in the snow and packed them down so hard that they didn't find them till the spring thaw. It didn't help that we couldn't remember where we had buried them. When we lived out at Raystown the snows used to get really deep. You would walk after a snowfall and find yourself covered in snow up to your boot tops.

We used to pull tricks and pranks on each other all the time whether it was my sister and our neighbor or myself pulling one on my sister. The best one I pulled on my sister was when we were both fighting over who was going to sit underneath the lawn chair. We didn't want to sit on the top of the lawn chair like most people do, but being kids, we wanted to sit underneath it. I won. Before long I felt something crawling all over me. I looked down and there were red ants crawling on me. I got them off of me and a smile came over my face for I had the grandest idea. I thought to myself this would be great.

I casually got up off the ground and walked over to my sister who was steaming but got sidetracked playing with her dolls. Janet hadn't seen me swishing the ants off myself. "Janet," I said. "Do you want to sit underneath the chair now?" "Why?" Janet asked. I told her I just didn't feel like it anymore. Janet said, "Yeah!" She was very excited about it. She went over to the chair and made herself comfortable under the lawn chair. I, on the other hand, sat patiently, watching and waiting. I snickered to myself about how brilliant I was. Suddenly, Janet jumped from the ground like she had been shot from a cannon. "MOM! MOM!" she cried. Mom ran out of the house to see what was wrong. My sister told her that I got her to sit on a pile of red ants as I tried to explain that I just didn't want to sit there anymore. I was laughing so hard that if I had had stitches (which I didn't), they would have burst open. That's probably why my mom didn't believe it was so innocent. I got in trouble and had to go in the house for the rest of the day. I hated it because I wanted to play outside.

Well, you may ask; was it worth it to me to get sent inside when I loved being outside? My answer would be, YES! It was funny, what can I say? I used to play a lot of tricks and pranks on my sister while we were young but believe me she has her own stories to tell, too. I can assure you when we talk about them now as we've gotten older we can laugh about all those dumb things we did as a young kids.

Our House at Raystown

Two Generations – Two Lives Saved
(Part 1)

At sixteen years old, Dr. Hodgeman, a heart specialist, at the Cleveland Clinic in Ohio told me if I didn't have heart surgery, and didn't have children, I would live to be forty years old. If I had children without the surgery, I would die having them. So, I elected to have the surgery right after graduation at seventeen. I had a hole in my heart and only two chambers were working instead of four.

I spent two weeks in the hospital, including the Fourth of July. Before being released I had to be up and around walking. After being released the doctor advised that I walk two miles a day. This is so your lungs keep expanded after surgery. I followed doctor's orders and went back for a yearly checkup. My surgery was successful enough to have children.

I had been dating my ex-husband (whom I would divorce ten years later) for three years before we decided to get married; I was just turning nineteen years old. We had our first child, Lucas, about ten months later. No sense waiting, since I really wanted to have children and felt blessed to be able to have them. Lucas' middle name is Lemonte, his dad's first name. Lucas weighed in at 8 lbs. 2 oz. and was almost bald, but I adored him. He was the cutest baby I had ever seen. All parents tend to say that.

Lucas was just over two years old when I became pregnant with my second child. The doctor said everything was fine and the baby was growing and developing just like it should be. I had bad feelings that something was wrong, or maybe my imagination was running wild. Maybe, I was worried for nothing. At three months, I couldn't shake the eerie feeling, but nothing indicated otherwise. It was just a sense that something wasn't right.

As the months passed, my baby was growing and developing. I was six months now and the doctor did an ultrasound on my belly to check the baby's vital signs. The doctor let me take the stethoscope and listen to the baby's heartbeat to reassure me everything was fine. I still had the gnawing feeling I had had since being three months pregnant. I had even had a conversation with my mom and my sister about it. They both thought if the doctor was telling me it was ok then it had to be.

Now, I was in my ninth month of the pregnancy. Still feeling uneasy and not really reassured by the doctor. I was definitely bigger in size but couldn't shake the awful feeling I was having. I got a check up to make sure I wasn't dilating. Everything checked out. Later on in the month, now nine and a half months pregnant, they checked me again. I seemed okay, but they said if I didn't have the baby within the week they would induce.

I was checked out on a Thursday and I'm not really sure why I remember so well the day of the week, but the days that soon followed would most likely explain it. That same Thursday night I lay in bed and started to feel the most awful pains. It wasn't like the normal birth pains and the doctor had told me everything was fine. She also told me that I would know when the baby was coming because my water would break. The pain would come and go, off and on, all weekend.

It was Monday morning and by now the pains were so awful I couldn't even move. I went to the doctors. After a nurse had checked me she said I was lucky to have come in when I did. I was in labor and dilated three centimeters. My water hadn't even broken or so I thought.

They wanted to see how the baby was so they hooked up the ultra sound to my belly. No heart beat! I was frightened and just knew that my worst fears were becoming reality. The mid-wife went to get one of the other baby delivery doctors to check me out. When the doctor came and examined me he had told me the baby had died inside of me. I wanted that ultra sound hook up off of me, and I told them to get it off of me or I would rip it off. The nurse disconnected it and took it off. I didn't need to listen to the silence that I knew had meant my baby was dead.

The doctors realized that they might have made a mistake telling me this beforehand. I still had to deliver my baby, and I knew it was dead inside me. So, when the next pains came they told me to push. Push I did because I was grasping at that one piece of a glimmer of hope that they were wrong, and my baby was alive.

After pushing and delivering my baby boy they confirmed that he had died over the weekend. They had told me it probably was Thursday night, the same day they checked me. I didn't have any water because they told me there must have been a small pinhole size where my water was leaking. And, instead of having my water break all at once, I had just thought it was a sign of having to go to the bathroom.

After I knew my baby was really dead, I didn't want to go on and I didn't care much about anything. All I could think of was my baby boy had died. The midwife kept telling me to push again, and I kept thinking to myself, why? I didn't want to live. I was at the point of willing myself to die along with my baby.

At this point I had to push. It had already been about 20 minutes and I had to get the after birth out now. If the afterbirth is not delivered in a certain amount of time, you risk dying on the table, or they literally have to go inside you with no medication to pull it out. The midwife had revealed this detail later to me in my recovery room. She had told me it is extremely painful.

As I was lying on the cold hard table and willing myself to go with my son, I could see the lights of the medical equipment and I could feel myself fading away. I could still hear a lot of the nurses and the doctor sounding like they were in a panic. They yelled to put a needle in my right arm to stop the bleeding. Then I heard someone yell; give her another one! I felt another needle in my left arm. At that point, I was hemorrhaging badly. Finally, a nurse yelled, "were losing her." I didn't care. I just wanted to be with my son. It seemed to last awhile. It felt like I was stuck in a movie with the hustle and bustle of a busy New York street with people running around me and talking. I didn't know what they were all chattering about, but I just wanted to go to sleep, and get some peace and quiet.

Another nurse came into the room. I didn't really know it so much until she came by my bedside and started to grab my arm and started to talk to me. I started to hear her say, "Barb don't go. You can't go! You have a son at home who needs you. What is he going to do without his mom? You have to stay here for him. I know it's hard but he's too young to not have a mom." Then a pause, and someone told her my son's name. I'm not really sure but it could have even been me for all I know. She started to talk again. "Barb, think about your son, Lucas. Think about Lucas! You have a three-year-old son who needs you to come home." I don't remember thinking about it much, but when she started to talk about Lucas, I started to will myself to come back to the real world.

Then I heard the mid-wife tell me; "You have to push! You have to push now!" So, I started to push. The afterbirth had started to get hard and it was bad to look at. Not the color it should have been. It was all purple and black. But, it was probably because it was inside of me for almost 3 or 4 days with no life attached. Lucas had saved my life. Who would have thought that a three year old, even though he wasn't there with me, could have saved my life? But, he did.

The next day the nursing staff asked me if I wanted to have some time with my son. I said, yes. They had him cleaned up and wrapped in a baby blanket. I had named my baby boy, Brock Mitchell. We didn't name him

93

after anyone in the family. We had just liked the name. Brock had lots of dark black hair and was so tiny. He had only weighed 3 lbs. 3 oz. His skin was purple. If he had lived, he might have had something wrong with him, but even though that may have been the case, I still would have wanted him with me. The staff of doctors told me he had the cord wrapped around his neck and that may have been why he died, but they also said because he was so tiny at full term, there was probably something else wrong. They asked me if I wanted an autopsy on him and I flatly refused. I wanted my baby to be left alone, and I didn't want them to do that to him. Later on, I would regret my decision. Now at times I still wonder what was wrong. Sometimes it eases one's mind to know the answers. I think Brock died Thursday night when I felt his little heart beating really rapidly inside of my belly and then nothing. If only I had known what was going on! If only I had had hindsight!

Losing my baby wasn't easy. For the next two years, I cried a lot and was out of touch with people. I did what I had to for my son Lucas, but felt lost inside. I hadn't wanted any more children after my stillbirth but after two years started to think about trying again so Luke would have someone to play with. I just was afraid of the same thing happening again. I started to realize after two years, I had to get on with my life for the sake of my son, Luke.

I had Mitchell, my third son, two years after the birth of Brock. I named him Mitchell, Brock's middle name. And, Mitchell's middle name, Anson, was named after me, meaning the son of Ann, my middle name. Lucas and Mitch are five years apart. Everything didn't go as planned with Mitch's birth either. The cord was wrapped around his body once and around his neck twice. I had to stop pushing so they could unwrap the cord. The doctors at this point had advised me that I should get my tubes tied. It was just too dangerous for me to have any more children. Not just for me, but also for the child I was carrying. I just had too many medical problems while carrying a baby. Mitch looked just like Brock when he was born. Lots of black hair but weighed in at 8 lbs. 8 oz. For a short time, I even accidentally called Mitch, Brock. I rectified that pretty quickly because I knew I had to.

Part 2

After I was able to do things again, I decided one day to take Lucas, now five, swimming at the Huntingdon swimming hole by the IGA. In the daytime the swimming area had lifeguards. Since Mitch was still a baby, he stayed at home with his dad. I wanted to take Lucas swimming to get him out and have some fun in our lives again. Lucas started to play in the sand with one of his friends. I was sitting beside him and a friend of mine said she would watch Lucas if I wanted to go into the water for a swim. I was hesitant, but decided it would be nice to cool down on such a hot day. She insisted that Lucas would be fine.

Before going into the water I told Lucas not to go any closer to the water zone where they didn't have buoys because it would be too deep for him. Unfortunately, the swimming area had been made too deep because people dammed it up with old boards to make it rise. A few people had gotten stuck in those boards over the years, and one had drowned.

So, away I went expecting my friend to watch my son like she promised, and Lucas knew what he was allowed to do and not to do. While I was in the water I spotted him walking away from the area I told him to stay in. I knew he was curious about the forbidden area. And, that's exactly where he was headed. The lifeguards didn't notice him and were still sitting in their tall chairs. A suntan seemed more important to them than watching for children going where they shouldn't.

I jumped out of the water and started to run toward Lucas. He jumped in as I was coming up behind him. I knew the water was way to deep for him so I didn't take time to yell for a lifeguard. To get to him I had to jump off the cement wall that supports the boards. So, I jumped! I was thinking to myself, I'm not a good swimmer, but I must save my son.

95

I got to Lucas as he was going under. He started to panic. I knew if he'd panic, he'd take us both under, and we would both drown. I grabbed him underneath his arms, and tried to keep him up, but he kept fighting me. I finally yelled at him "Luke, don't panic! Relax! If you don't, you are going to take us both under. Stop and just let me take you to shore." Lucas at that point realized he had to stay calm and listen to me or we weren't going to make it ashore. After pulling him in, I realized I had scraped my big toe. I had a big chunk of skin out of it. My friend apologized, but I didn't want to hear it. We got our belongings and headed home. I had to calm down from this frightening ordeal and take care of my toe. I told Lucas from now on when I tell him something he must listen. It's not that I don't want him to have fun, but sometimes I must protect him from dangerous situations.

That day I pulled Lucas from the water and saved his life, just as he had saved my life when I lost Brock. Thank God we were both there for each other.

Corning
(Bad for My Health)

I started working at Corning in 1989 about a year after I got divorced. I had two young children that I raised on my own. I moved to a trailer out by Whipple Dam. Turned out no one in Huntingdon wanted to rent to anyone who knew my ex-husband. I was about a half hour from my work. I hated working swing shift, but the money was good and raising two kids on my own, I needed it. Swing shift consisted of working 7 am to 3 pm, 3 pm to 11 pm and 11 pm to 7 am. Normally, I'd work seven days in a row, have two off, another seven with two off, and then seven with a four day long weekend.

I usually had to pay the babysitter half of my check, but thought eventually as my children grew older I would be able to get us some nice things when they'd one day be able to stay there by themselves. They were just too young now.

At first I was afraid in the trailer being secluded in the woods but after awhile I started to get used to it. The boys and I went to the humane society to pick out a new dog, and now and then we'd see some wild animals. A bear was out by our mailbox one day. However, my fear was, that one of my children would be walking home and see one of those bears with her cubs. The other time I was feeding a skunk out my front porch. It trusted me as I was feeding it every morning with some bread and milk and I trusted the skunk not to spray me. This was one of my favorite animals.

Corning brought on some real health issues for me. The first incident happened with my feet. They had metal grating you had to stand on at times and my smaller toes started to go underneath my feet. I could hardly walk out of there some days. We had to wear steel-toed shoes, safety glasses and earplugs. I don't think the steel-toed shoes helped my feet any. I went to get a check up with the foot doctor and he told me I'd have to have both feet operated on. I choose not to do them at the same time so I could take care of my children. The first surgery was for a bunion and hammertoes, which was done in the morning. I followed the doctor's orders, kept it propped up and had little problems. About four months later, I had the other foot operated on for the same things. The surgeon breaks them, straightens it and then you have to just wait for them to heal. The second time I was in a lot of pain. I was operated on in the afternoon. Not sure if that had something to do with the pain I was in, but I believe the doctor's are more rested in the morning. That's my opinion anyway.

After my foot problem was resolved, a few years later I got cut while taking pins out of glass on television screens. We had to rivet the pins out of the glass if there were flaws in them and then they'd get recycled back. Even though I always wore my protective arm guards, the one time the glass exploded and it went into my wrist. The glass cut my artery in half, my tendons, and the nerves in my left hand. I had absolutely zero strength in my hand. The doctor told me if I was going to get cut he wished it had been on the other side of my hand. I got cut on the side of my two smaller fingers where my pinky finger is. This is the side, he said, where your strength comes from in your hand to open jars and things like that. But, I didn't have a choice. If I had had a choice, I wouldn't have gotten cut at all.

When this kind of thing happens you learn new ways of doing things. While my hand was healing, I had to do the dishes. My boys were still very young. I would set a plate down on the counter; hold it with my elbow and wash one side, rotate, and then the other. It was very frustrating to cut my fingernails on my right hand since I had no strength at all in my left one. I would sit the clippers on the counter, put my nail in the clipper where I wanted to cut it and then push the clipper down with my elbow. Dressing was another experience. It was very hard to get dressed with jeans, so I wore mostly dresses for a while. When going to the bathroom, it would seem like my arm was like a log, just in the way and heavy. Something you had to deal with because it was there. I would

98

literally rest my arm on the sink counter and deal with my clothes with my other hand. I had to pick up my arm and rest it down like it was separate from me.

After about six weeks of healing, I started therapy. I had to do simple things like trying to make my fingers go in to touch each other and pulling putty off of a ball. This was all the strength I could muster. After awhile I got up to squeezing a ball and eventually doing wrist curls and rubber band exercises. My two fingers had to be trained to lay flat because at first they wouldn't. They were bent and I had to wear a splint for a while. My hand is still not 100%, not even 60%. My pinky finger and half of my ring finger, along with part of my hand down to my wrist are always numb. In the winter I have to keep my hand warm, as it gets very cold. I regained about 40 to 50% strength in my hand. The doctor told me to be careful lifting weights and things because sometimes my hand will lock up. While cooking and holding onto a bowl to scrap out the contents it will lock up on me sometimes, and then I can hardly hold onto it. I just have to put it down and shake out my hand till it goes back to what I call my "normal".

I got married to my second husband, John, in 1993. In 1995, I was still working at Corning when something else happened. I was at work one day and my lip had a tingling feeling in it. I thought a bug had bitten me. As the day went on, I started to feel funny, so I asked to go home. After leaving, I went home and later on that night my face on the one side went numb. I told my husband I was scared and feared I was having a stroke. John took me to the emergency room. My face was drooping on the one side and upon examination the doctor also thought the same thing. Then all of a sudden he realized that it was something else with my nerves in my face. He sent me to a neurologist to confirm his suspicions. I had developed Bells Palsy. I had never even heard of it before. The doctor said it's a virus in the environment that attacks and affects your nerves. He said there was nothing I could do about it except let it run its course. There were five people at Corning that got it around the same time as I did. It's not contagious. Workers were digging inside the plant at the time and a lot of lead dust was floating in the air. The doctor believes that's how we got it.

I couldn't close my left eye at all, so at night I had to put a patch on it and tape it shut. This was so the eye wouldn't get scratched while sleeping, and to try and keep it somewhat moist. Usually in the middle of the night, the eye would pop open and it would burn from the tape touching it. I would jump out of bed and rip it off. Then I'd have to wake my poor husband up to have him help me retape it. I would have to put eye drops in my eye at least four times a day to keep my eye from drying out. Sometimes it can go the other way where people have an eye that closes and can't open it. At least when I was awake, it didn't look like I was going around winking at everyone.

The other bad thing with Bells Palsy is when you talk your mouth goes to one side. So it looks weird when you're talking. I couldn't drink from a straw at all. If I did it would just drip, and spill down all over me. I never liked going out in public when I had Bells Palsy. It felt like everyone was staring at me. John, the boys, and I played a lot of games at the house those months till I got better. I went out one time to a restaurant. It was so embarrassed eating and the fact I felt like I was being stared at, I told John I wouldn't be going out anymore. He was understanding, and stayed at home with me playing board games like Yahtzee, Scrabble and Scattergories. It took about four months for it to go away so I could go back to work. I was lucky that mine went away. The doctor said, sometimes it doesn't fully heal and some people live with at least some of their symptoms the rest of their lives. He said anyone can get it at any time and it can return with a virus in the air. The doctor told me someone he treated had it three times.

The only time I could laugh about it was at one of my routine checkups with the company doctor. I had to be able to close my eye the whole way for safety issues to be able to go back to work. The one day he told me to close my eye. I closed my right eye. This doctor never smiled or laughed and always looked like he was in a bad mood. He was the very serious type. Well, he wanted me to close my left eye, which was the eye that I couldn't close. He said; "no you goof, your bad eye." I told him, "Well, it's easier to close my good eye." He got such a big laugh out of that that day. I tried to close my left eye but it still wouldn't close the whole way and had to wait a few more weeks to get checked out again. The nurse told me that I put that doctor in a good mood all day and he was good to work around. She said he'd just start laughing out loud at times thinking of it. I told her; "I'm glad I could do you a favor." We both laughed.

A week before I got Bells Palsy, I enrolled in a Dale Carnegie class that I had wanted to take for along time. The company was paying for it. I felt sorry for myself for a week and didn't go. I decided I wasn't going to let sorry keep me from taking this class. The next day I went. I had to stand up before the class to speak. I'm not a good speaker in front of a group. I felt terrible and decided to tell everyone the truth. I told them I felt sorry for myself and that's why I wasn't there for a week, but I refused to give up a class I had wanted to take for over a year to Bells Palsy. The class is somewhere around $1,500 to take, and with two young children, my husband and I buying a new house, there was no way we could have afforded to pay for this. The class all stood up, clapped for me and said I had strength to have come back. Some of them said they were still not sure they would have come to the class. I wanted that class more than letting the Bells Palsy have all that power over me.

After this incident with the Bells Palsy, my husband told me that was the last straw. He told me I needed to quit because there were just too many health problems that surrounded this job. He was definitely right. I knew a lot of people it seemed after they retired they would develop cancer or some other health problem. I am glad I am out of there. I didn't want any more health problems. No amount of money is worth it. I had worked there seven years before I left that job. The plant closed its doors after several more years down the road, not because of health issues with employees, but because they could no longer sell as many glass products with televisions as they once had. People moved on to find other jobs in the area or moved away. I'm not sure however, I would have quit as easily if it had not been for the Dale Carnegie class. They teach you how to go after what you want and to go after your goals. I learned a lot from that class and at the end I got a huge surprise.

I received the Dale Carnegie highest achievement award. I would have never suspected that in a million years that they were going to vote for me. I also didn't realize how big of a deal it is to get until the instructor told us what this award means. My husband came to watch me speak the last night because they tell you to invite family members when you complete the course. They had called him ahead of time and told him I was getting this award. He never whispered a peep of it to me. He told me afterward though he was so proud of me. I had pushed past the Bells Palsy and took the class anyway and had decided to quit my job at Corning because of health issues, along with the fact I hated swing shift. I was miserable there.

I went on to take a photography class at Lock Haven University and started my own business doing weddings. I found out I didn't like doing wedding photography. I worked at American Studios, which is in Wal-Mart, for about six months. Although I love taking pictures, I hated the hours there and started to learn secretarial/receptionist skills. I learned I could do whatever I set my mind to do, and if I don't like something, I can just move on. Life's too short to worry about stuff. There are plenty of jobs out there that don't affect your health as much as Corning did mine.

Licorice
(A piece of candy or just sweet?)

About six months after our dog Flash died, I asked my husband if he would mind if I got a skunk. I had wanted one since I was a child, but just never knew where to get one. He said he didn't mind, so I did some research on the Internet. The breeder took care of the permits you need by law to own a skunk. You are required to carry the permit with you at all times while traveling with your skunk. Some states do not allow you to keep exotic animals, so if you are traveling out of Pennsylvania, and are stopped by the police without your skunk permit, they are allowed to confiscate your animal. The veterinarian also needs this permit in order to treat a skunk and to know that it has been domesticated. After calling around State College and getting turned down numerous times, I finally found a veterinarian who was willing to do checkups. The doctor from the Mt. Nittany Animal Veterinary Hospital near Lemont, said, "I like a new challenge." He had never treated skunks before, but agreed to take care of the vet needs. After finding a vet, I headed to York to pick out my new pet.

When I arrived in York, Brad, the breeder, told John and me to follow him to the barn where he had 250 skunks to choose from. Brad and his wife had rescued all these skunks from a man who was breeding them in Canada. They rented a medium sized U-Haul truck to carry all the skunks back to Pennsylvania, but in spite of the size of the U-Haul, Brad and his wife still had to make several trips. Canada had passed a new law prohibiting exotic animals as pets. The law made it clear that the breeder in Canada must put them all to sleep or let someone from another state where it is legal to have exotic animals come and take them away. Once they are domesticated they would never be able to survive in the woods. No one is allowed to extract skunks from the wild and keep as pets. They must come from a licensed breeder who has domesticated them and had them vaccinated for rabies.

Since there are no vaccinations specifically for a skunk, they have to use a dog rabies shot. Even though you get your skunk vaccinated, if they bite someone, and that person goes to the hospital, animal control can come to your house and take your skunk to make sure it doesn't have rabies. The only way they can check for rabies is to kill the animal. There is an underground skunk ring where people who love and care for these animals, will come and pick up the skunk at your house, if need be, and take care of them. They will care for the animal until it is safe for the animal to go home, so they will not to be killed. They will actually take the animal state-to-state, house-to-house, to protect them. Luckily, for me I never had to use their service. I would have never put anyone's life in danger for an animal, no matter how much I love the animal.

When I got to York to pick out my skunk, Brad told me I could pick out a rescue for $20.00 or one of his for $350.00. The rescues were all spayed or neutered and descented. Brad had to find homes for all of them. He also didn't know what kind of personalities they would have since he didn't raise them and the breeder in Canada had abused them. The Canadian breeder left the skunks in their cages while cleaning them, and that scared them to death. The skunks would have to try and dodge a powerful water hose. He also would pick them up by their tail and just hold them if he needed to check them out for anything. I'm not sure why he did it this way, other than it seemed he never really cared too much for the skunks he raised. He was only in the business to make a buck. He treated them like varmints instead of pets.

Domesticated skunks come in all colors; there are silver backs, pure white ones that look like big rats with bushy tails, brown and white ones, white skunks with black strips, black skunks with white strips, spotted ones, and reddish colored skunks. You don't get all this variety of colors out in the woods. Every now and then, you may be lucky enough to come across a white skunk but they are rare.

After looking over all the skunks, I choose a two-year old female rescue with the traditional black and white strip. I had wanted the black and

104

white even as I sat in school as a child. I would sit in class and let my mind wonder and think of names for my skunk. I named her Licorice. I had known the name of my skunk for years.

When I got Licorice home, my husband and I had to work with her a lot to get her to the point that we could pick her up enough to cut her nails. She would also pace back and forth over our heat register because of the long narrow pen where she lived in Canada. After months of working with her, she stopped pacing the register. It took over a year to get her to the point she trusted us enough to lie down on our lap. She never liked to be held.

Licorice would try to scare us away at first by raising her tail, stomping, and then she'd drag her front paws while backing up. When she'd raise her tail, she would make it fan out like a peacock and it was beautiful. She could stare at you and have her butt pointed at you at the same time, like an accordion. Normally, this is a scare tactic, and in the wild they will spray you. She used it on us until she got to trust us. After she trusted us, she stopped doing it. We actually missed it because it was so cute to see her tail fanned out so eloquently. Skunks normally will not spray you even in the wild unless they really feel threatened. This may be because it takes them a long time to rejuvenate their spray. I had read up on how to take care of skunks and how they live.

Skunks make wonderful pets when you raise them from a baby. Personally, I believe they make better pets than a cat. If you are allergic to cats, then skunks are for you. I am allergic to cats but not skunks. The reason most people are allergic to cats isn't because of their dander, it's because of the saliva. Cats lick themselves, and hair falls from their coats. If you are allergic to the saliva, you will get it on you, and have an allergic reaction. I was going to get a hairless cat one time and the lady wouldn't sell me one unless I was tested for the saliva. This is backed up by science. As for skunks, they don't lick themselves except their paws after a meal. They have coarser hair, even though it is soft, and they have no saliva on it when it falls out. They rarely shed and this makes for a cleaner environment in your home. Skunks on average live about twelve years, but have been known to live up to twenty years with a healthy diet.

A healthy diet for a skunk is exactly like what a human being would consider healthy eating. You need lots of vegetables, a few pieces of chicken or egg now and then, some fruit, skunks like grapes, and some good vitamins if they are not getting enough in their diet. You can get a recipe from a skunk chat site on the Internet called, "Skunkie Delight." Skunkie Delight consists of healthy food mixes that you can get at a health food store with vitamins mixed in. If you are going to feed them regular dog or cat food, dog food is better, but it has to have no preservatives in it. The preservatives sometimes will make them have itchy skin. They only need a bath about once every three months. Too many baths can cause their skin to get flaky. Getting the right vitamins from foods can keep their coat looking silky and shinny.

Skunks are intelligent animals, but if you do them wrong, they don't forget easily and it may take awhile for them to forgive you. They will go to the bathroom in a litter box. To get them litter trained, you have to set the box in a corner. They prefer a corner. A little bit of privacy please! If they were out in the woods, they would back up to a tree to do their business. If you don't want the litter box in the corner you first selected, you have to start in the corner, then slowly, inch by inch, day by day, move the litter box slowly to where you want it to be. Licorice rarely ever went on the floor. If she was out in the family room playing and needed to go to the bathroom, she would go right in her room to the litter box. As long as you keep the litter box cleaned out, skunks will use it. On average, they only do number two twice a day, so it can be cleaned easily with a scupper.

Licorice had her own little room set up. She slept in her pet carrier that had a roof on it. It created more of a den feel. I never locked her in, so she could come in and out of her room as she pleased. Skunks can also be trained to come out more in the daytime. You just need to work with them and get them up everyday when you want them to be out. Licorice was up everyday in the middle of the afternoon playing. She had an attitude that the house was hers and you were there to serve her. Just like other animals, they all have different personalities.

Normally, you can take skunks with you for car rides, but in Licorice's case, she didn't like other people, so I was unable to do that with her. You can train them when they are little to wear a harness like the ones made for ferrets. Because Licorice had been abused for up to two years before I got her, I wasn't able to get a harness on her.

Licorice became a sweet little girl but she was missing companionship. I had to go to work full time and couldn't spend a lot of time with her. I had had Licorice for close to five years, but she started to get bored and seemed to be unmotivated at times to play. Skunks need a lot of stimulation. To keep Licorice busy I had given her her own garbage can with shredded newspapers in it, along with some food. She would then work to tip the can over and dig for the food. I also had cat toys for her, but she soon got bored with those.

It took me nearly six months to finally make the decision to give her away. After awhile, I just knew I had to find her a home with other skunks. I wasn't able to spend much time with Licorice, and I didn't want to get another skunk that I also couldn't spend a lot of time with. I found a couple on the Internet from South Carolina that I interviewed. This is another state that allows residents to have skunks with a permit, so I let them take Licorice. It was really hard to give her up but I knew she would have a good home. I did it for her, putting my feelings aside. I knew she needed the companionship or she would go down hill. The family who adopted her had nineteen skunks of their own. All of their skunks lived inside the house, and Licorice made number twenty. Skunks are this family's whole life and they don't spend time away from home, so that made them the perfect couple to care for Licorice.

I keep in contact with the South Carolina family to check up on Licorice. She adjusted well to the other skunks, which is what she needed. The family will email pictures of their skunks, and I can tell right away which one is Licorice. Most of the time, Licorice is pictured in their kitchen with at least ten of her little skunk buddies surrounding her. It wasn't best for me to give her up, but it was best for her. I knew that. In the future, I know I will get a pair of skunks to add to the family, but it will have to be when I am sure I have quality time to give them.

If you are ever thinking of getting a skunk, you should read up on their care first to make sure this pet is for you. I knew all about them before I got Licorice, but like I said, I had wanted one ever since I was a young child.

Marshmallow Anyone?

Where were you on 9-1-1?

September 11, 2001, better known as 9-1-1. I was at work when the devastation, chaos, fear and anguish took place all around New York and Pennsylvania. At work everyone was glued to the radio, listening for reports and the looking at it on the Internet.

The news had been reporting that planes had been taken over by hijackers and flown into The World Trade Center, better known as The Twin Towers. When the first tower was hit, people were told to stay put in the second tower. That would later be regretted in a big way. Right after the first plane hit tower one, the second plane was going to hit tower two. The devastation would be overwhelming. Thousands of people had lost their lives; family members crushed by their losses. Everything around New York was in shambles. People were screaming and running out of the towers with black smoke everywhere, while firemen and police were running in to try and save lives. My co-workers and I were in disbelief. Everyone glued to his or her spots. How could this be happening? And...Why?

One of my co-workers kept pacing back and forth, she was in her early twenties and even though she didn't know anyone in New York, she had the look of terror in her eyes. One co-worker actually had someone he knew who worked in the towers and was trying to find out if he was okay. A few days later he would find out that the gentleman he knew had gotten out safely. One person survived out of thousands who weren't as lucky.

Later on, that same day we heard of another plane which had been taken over and flying over Pennsylvania on it's way to Washington, DC. The passengers were calling loved ones on their cell phones to tell them good-bye and that they weren't just sitting back and waiting to die. They were going to do something. They had decided to try and take back the plane. After being told by loved ones that the two planes had hit the twin towers, there was no going back. They made a stand with the hijackers but the plane went down in a field. All had been killed; they were our heroes. That day they saved another tragedy from happening in Washington, but it still left family members mourning.

My husband came home to tell me he had to prepare enough clothes for three days in case they had to spend their time away from home. All State Troopers were called to report, and had to be on standby in case they were needed. They were preparing for a lot more destruction and devastation. Some troopers reported to the airports to check baggage and passengers coming in, others were stationed elsewhere around the area and preparing for riots or other problems arising.

I was overwhelmed with fear and grief. Fear that I may lose my husband and family members and grief for the people who were already killed in all the senseless taking of their lives. How could the United States recover? A lot of people were wondering, and fear was all around them. There was a tighter closeness of family that some people hadn't felt in a long time. People were pulling together and keeping their family closer. The little things that seemed to matter didn't matter anymore.

The people of the United States came together like they hadn't done in years. People were helping each other out. Survival kicked in. Others reached out and settled up their differences. People had a new sense of patriotism and togetherness. Flags were sold out from all the stores; people hung them from their homes, their cars, and mailboxes, and wherever they could put them. The sense of pride for our country was overwhelming. Men and women signed up for the military to defend our country. The recruiting stations hadn't had this number of volunteers in a long time. People had pride and it showed. They were ready to fight for our freedom and get the bastards who did this to our country.

My son was one of those boys who had signed up for the military. He had enlisted in the Marines. When he graduated from Parris Island, SC we were all very proud of him, but also scared. At least three or four of his friends had also signed up. The president gave an address to the troops on Thanksgiving Day in 2003 when he went to Baghdad, Iraq. My son wasn't in Baghdad when the President was there, but I had added the address to my son's military album. President Bush stated that attacks on the United States and on our freedom would not be tolerated. He also stated that the terrorist would be caught and punished.

A year or so later after 9-1-1, Pennsylvania made a memorial for the people who were on the plane that went down in Shanksville. A lot of books were written on the subject, and one of the passengers from the plane that went down in Pennsylvania wrote a book called: "Let's Roll". A wife of one of the passengers named the book after the statement she had heard from her husband while on the phone when the passengers were talking about taking over the hijackers. I haven't read the book but someday I would like to. I believe they have erected a memorial in New York as well where the Twin Towers had stood. A movie has also been released in May 2006 about the tragedy, called: Flight United 93.

I remember talking to my son, Mitch, on the phone in December of 2004 when the news came across on the television that Saddam Hussein had been caught for torturing all those people in Iraq. Mitch was stationed at Camp Geiger, Jacksonville, NC. You could hear all the cheering, the Ooh Rah's! and the joy in the background from our troops. It was so loud I could barely hear my son on the phone. He was relaying what was on TV to the guys in the barracks.

End Note:
Hopefully a tragedy never happens like this again, but I'm not so sure it won't the way things look in our world now-a-days. I just hope we always have our freedom, and I wish that all of the military personal that are fighting for our country come home safely. So I ask; "Where were you on 9-1-1?" Do you remember?

(I wrote this about a month after this tragedy happened.)

What do you want to be when you grow up?

Do you remember people asking you; what do you want to be when you grow up? As I was growing up I can remember always wanting to pursue different careers and do certain things. Let me tell you about what I wanted to be, and why or why not I didn't pursue them.

I remember when I was in first grade wanting to be a math teacher. In grade school I loved working with numbers, and I enjoyed it too until algebra came into the picture. That sort of put a damper on things so I gave up that dream. I figured if you want to do the math you would also have to learn algebra in college and well that wasn't for me. So on to the next goal.

I also had the dream of flying my own airplane. Not many people know this about me. My first time flying was when I was in my late teens and I got to know someone who had his own plane. We took off the ground and while in the air, the pilot did a 180-degree turn. I believe that's what they call it when you do a flip in the air. I loved it! He showed me all those gauges and gadgets they have on those planes and that would make anyone's head spin. No pun intended. Even though I still love to fly in an airplane I will let that up to someone else.

My next dream was to be a veterinarian. I love animals, and it would be so nice to work with animals, and to me that would have been the most distressful job I could have. Until, I realized one day after sleeping on feather pillows I was allergic to birds. Well, I could probably still be a veterinarian, but not treat birds. Right? Wrong. I soon discovered over the years that I was allergic to cats and severely. I wasn't always that way. There was a chemical leak where I lived at the time from some old tanks buried in the ground, and it made my lungs more sensitive to everything. I am also allergic to horses, guinea pigs and a lot of other furry creatures. I found out first hand after buying guinea pigs for my own children that I was having a hard time breathing while I changed their pen. There was one thing I could have had even though I personally didn't want them, and that was a hermit crab. I bought each one of my boys their own and since they are none shedders so to speak. (Hermit crabs shed one shell as they get bigger and move out to get another one a little bigger). So, whoa-la! No shedding, no problem. But, they weren't for me. I don't really think I could make a business out of just treating hermit crabs. One day we ended up having no heat in our house and I had to take my children to my moms to stay until it was fixed. When we went back I discovered that the hermit crabs were frozen. I forgot to take them with us. It was sad for my boys and I felt really bad but there was nothing I could do.

I also wanted to become a photographer, and I have taken some classes on the subject. I love taking pictures. I tried my hand at weddings, but to me personally, it was boring sitting there waiting for the in between stuff to be over so I could take my pictures. However, I still love taking pictures but for my own personal use. I do a lot of scrapbooking as a hobby, so in a way I have pursued this somewhat.

The last career I wanted as I was growing up was writing. I still am hoping to pursue this more. I love to write but just need to perfect it and try to pick something in the field that interests me. When I read, I tend to go toward non-fiction and biographies, with just a little fiction thrown in.

As you can see, I haven't been able to fulfill all of my dreams, or even half of them you might say. But I have enjoyed my life so far with my children, grandchildren and my husband. When I get time for myself, I can always try to figure out what I want to be when I grow up. Later.

The Park

It was around noon, on Friday, April 28, 2006. My husband, John ("Pap" to Landon) and I decided to take Landon to Spring Creek Park by Lemont. The sky was clear blue, a chilly day, temperature in the low sixties, the sun was shining bright enough to make you squint without sunglasses, and a slight breeze blowing. From the parking area, we walked right into the park where there is a sandbox area. There was a little girl digging in the sand but Landon didn't want to do any digging there today.

His first stop was getting on the frog, a toy like ride that swings back and forth that he straddled like riding a horse, not like a regular swing you sit on. Then it was off to the rocket ship, same type of ride like the frog. After a few times of this Landon headed to the sliding boards. Walking up the ladder and then an exciting slide down, again and again.

Landon spotted the creek, glanced at Pap and me, and away he went. Pap and Landon were picking up rocks and throwing stones to see who could make the biggest splash. While reaching down to touch the water, Landon's left foot slipped on the side of the bank and got wet, along with his left pant leg. Or, was the slip pre-planned by a three year old who loves playing in the water? Hmm. We didn't want him to get wet and had to go to the car to change his socks and pants. Usually an extra set of clothing is a good thing to carry with you with a three year old.

Landon wanted something to drink, so I drove to Sheetz while the boys (Pap and Landon) stayed at the park to play. When I returned with orange sodas for Landon and Pap and a Diet Pepsi for myself, we sat at the picnic table to drink them. After the drinks were gone it was back for some more play time. Landon traced his steps again with a ride on the frog, the rocket, a few times down the sliding board, a walk across the covered bridge and then back playing by the creek.

Pap and Landon were sitting by the creek and Landon was making a hole in the dirt with his hands, seeing how deep he could get it. They both sat and watched the water rippling while throwing rocks in. Landon had his Altoona Curve hat on just like Pap. Anything Pap does, Landon does. They both wore jeans, sneakers and sweatshirts. The only difference was the colors of the sweatshirt and sneakers. Landon had a red shirt and Pap a blue shirt, Pap's sneakers were the classic white and Landon's were blue spider-man style.

As I sat and watched everyone, a bee buzzed by my head, a butterfly flew past, and a plane went over the park. There was a lot happening in the air. My attention turned to a little girl who was playing near the swings. She only had a T-shirt on, underwear, no pants and no socks or shoes. The little girl was probably around four years old and looked chilled with her bare feet sticking out. I looked at John and said: "Don't people think about how they dress a child when it's chilly outside?" The mother, however, had on a sweatshirt, pants, socks and shoes. At least she was warm, I thought. It was too chilly out to have a child running around dressed like it was summertime.

As my attention turned onto something else, I noticed a man in his thirties standing by the tennis courts watching a game being played by two men around the same age. He was standing there for a while holding onto his cooler. I wondered why he didn't set it down. Oh well, maybe he didn't want anyone taking it. A lady with her two children broke my thought when she stopped to ask, "May I ask where you got your son's shoes?" We told her it was our grandson and proceeded to tell her, Wal-Mart. She then asked; "How much did you pay for them?' She was interested because they were spider-man shoes that light up in the toe and on the sides when Landon walks. Around $10.00, I replied. I didn't mind the asking. Her one boy was around the same age as Landon. She thanked me and walked away, trying to catch up to her children.

John told me, if I wanted to read for a while, he'd play with Landon.

When Pap's around, Landon wants to play with his "Ole Buddy Pal", as he calls Pap from time to time. I went to the car to grab a book and walked over the covered bridge to a quiet area where I could sit on a bench and still see Pap and Landon by the water. I noticed the smell of the crisp air and the soft scent of flowers beside me when the wind blew. Above in the trees, was the sound of birds chirping and singing their tunes. Dandelions were everywhere in the grass and there was a huge open area behind me where I noticed a couple with their golden retriever. The dog was running around as he enjoyed the freedom of no leash.

It was really peaceful just sitting and watching everything around me. I really couldn't get into reading my book. I just wanted to see how much I could really notice and take in. I could see parents sitting at a picnic table talking while watching their children playing on the playground equipment. A jogger went by, and at the same time you could hear a mother yelling at her children to stay put, and not run ahead of her. They didn't listen. They were around six to eight years old and she had to run to catch up to them. I could see her face getting angry and as she caught up to them, she scolded them. A few ducks floated by in the creek and Landon yelled across the water for me to see them. Two children came by John and Landon to kick a few rocks in the water. I couldn't hear Landon any longer across the creek because a man on a lawn mower was mowing the grass in the wide space behind me. I noticed there wasn't anyone playing on the volleyball court. There was no life there, but plenty of life going on around me.

We had been at the park for about two hours and John motioned to me that it was time to go. Landon would stay forever if he could, but had given in when Pap told him our dog Tucker would need us home. As I gathered up my belongings and headed back over the covered bridge to the park area, I noticed two young girls asking their dad to push them on the swings. A lady walked past with her little Yorkshire, and as I got to the parking lot, three men were standing by their car discussing work.

There's a lot to see and hear at a park, but also a chance to sit, relax, soak up some sun, and just enjoy the day. If you listen closely you can hear crying of toddlers not wanting to leave, parents yelling for their children to slow down or listen, but most of all, you can hear the laughter of children having fun.

Bridge at Spring Creek

The Bucket List:

Definition: Things you want to do before you kick the bucket.

Note: I thought this would be a good way to end my book. I can reflect back and see if any of these are accomplished.

Have you've seen the movie "The Bucket List?" We saw this movie on Saturday, January 12, 2008. It's with Morgan Freeman and Jack Nicholson. It's about two men who have illnesses and they only have so long to live. They decide to make a list of things they want to do before they "kick the bucket." Have you ever thought about what you'd like to do, or accomplish before you kick the bucket?

Here are a few of the things on my list. As I was writing this book, I have crossed off the things I already have done.

-See my grandson grow up.
-Visit Scotland, and find out more about my Gr. Gr. Grandmother Jesse Bruce. *(Of course, if I had the money to do this, I would have done it already.)*
-Travel all over the world. *(Over the years we have already visited about a dozen states.)*
-Go on a cruise.
~~-Write my memoirs. (The first half of my life.)~~
- Write my memoirs (The second half of my life.)
-Write my family history for my children, and grandchildren.
-Get all my photos into albums.
~~-Publish a book with my sister.~~
- Learn to scuba dive.

What about you? What's on your list?

Scrapbook Ideas

♣ ♦ ♥ ♠

One of my hobbies is doing scrapbooking. I love it! I started scrapbooking around the year 2000, and have been an avid scrapbooker every since.

I had the "Gift Album" and "Colors of The Crayons" ideas published in "The Scrapbook Club Bulletin." The issue numbers are toward the end of the book under credits.

I just thought I'd share them with you, and if you're a scrapbooker, you know just what I'm talking about.

Enjoy!

Scrapbook Supplies

Gift Album
(Scrapbook Album Idea)

For a gift album, write to family members, co-workers and friends and ask them to write a funny story or memory of the person you're making the album for. Ask them to include a picture of themselves with family and/or friends. Then, put their photo with their letter on your pages. This makes for a more personal gift than asking for a picture of whom you are making the gift for.

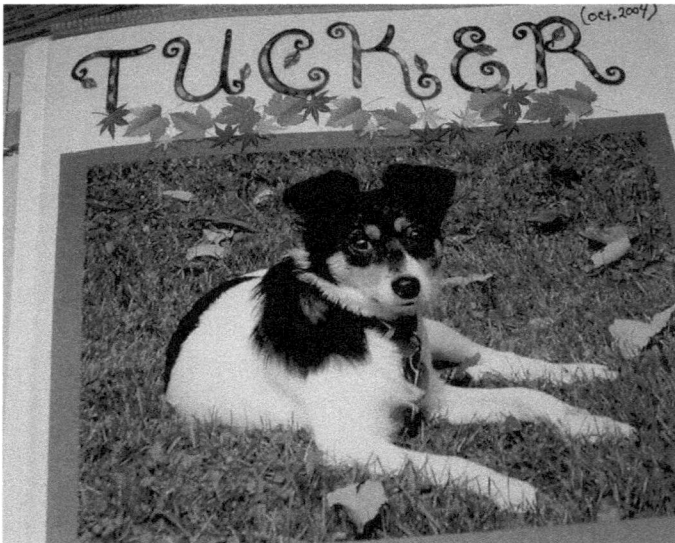

Our Dog Tucker's Album (Photo taken in 2004)

Colors of the Crayons

Do an album with the eight basic colors of crayons. There are many other possibilities, but here are some examples:

Red: embarrassed, mad, strawberries
Orange: fall colors, pumpkin
Yellow: afraid, playing in the sun
Green: playing in the grass, green with envy
Blue: blue jeans, feeling blue, water
Purple: a bruise, playing with Barney
Brown: playing in the mud, Brownie troop
Black: nighttime photo, black cat

Colors of the Crayons

Deck of Cards
(Scrapbook Idea)

Buy a regular deck of cards from your local store. Then add quotes, sayings, bible verses, or photos to the cards. You can find double-sided sticky tape at your local craft store. Punch a hole on each corner and add a ring to it. You can find these at your local office supply store.

They make wonderful gifts. You could do a 52-week of yourself or anything that stood out to you that week. Pick one day out of the week and do a 52 weeks of the weather, or do what you did that day everyday on the same day for 52 weeks. The possibilities are endless.

Tip: If doing photos on your cards, they stick better if you use a little sand paper first on your card to rough up the smooth surface.

Enjoy!

Bonus Idea

Marshmallow Snowman

My grandson, Landon, age five, came up with this idea. This would be great for children's parties for them to make. It's easy and fun.

Take three marshmallows, and add a toothpick in the middle to hold together. Then add some licorice to make the arms and legs. Landon used pieces of chocolate for the eyes and mouth. Then just find a small sized felt hat at a craft store to put on his head.

Everything is edible except the toothpick and hat.

Marshmallow Snowman

Photo Section

Attachments

The Boys At Christmas (2007)
Landon, Luke, and Mitch

My Dad When He Was In the Korean War
(Photo taken August 1950)
Richard H. Cresswell
National Guard Transportation Company
131st – 2nd Platoon
Huntingdon, PA

Mom in the 1950s
(Betty Cresswell)
While dad was in military he had this photo painted of my mom.

Both photos when we were younger living at Raystown.

Richard (My brother)

Barb (age 3), and Janet (sister, age 5)

Landon's Dandelion Pocket (2008)

Vacation
Myrtle Beach, SC
June 2008

Relaxing on the Beach

Sunrises on the beach

John and I took Landon to Myrtle Beach, SC.
So he could see the ocean.

Landon's Favorites:

Making Sandcastles
(This one is a candy sandcastle at one of the stores.)

Looking for seashells at the beach

Gator-Land

Swimming
(Although, Landon likes the pool better for swimming.)
And…

Mini-golfing

This was Landon's (age 5) first time when playing mini-golf,
that he made holes in one, twice.
His favorite mini-golf course was the one with
the dinosaurs with the T-Rex.

They have some wonderful mini-golf courses at Myrtle Beach.

I got a wonderful photo opportunity when I caught this bird catching a fish right when I snapped my photo.

Fresh Catch of the Day
Myrtle Beach, SC
June 2008

Book and Other Credits:
*(I have either published the book,
and/or my work has been included in the publication.)*

•

"The Weeping Rose"
Author: Janet L. Foster
Photographer: Barbara A. Foley
ISBN # 978-0-6152-1440-5
Published by Barb Foley
Printed by Lulu
To purchase this book:
Go to: http://stores.lulu.com/bfoley

•

"Endless Journeys"
Published by:
The International Library of Photography
Photographs: Barbara Foley
ISBN# 0-7951-5247-7
To purchase this book
Go to: www.picture.com

•

"The Scrapbook Club Bulletin"
Published by The Scrapbook Club
"Members' Corner"
Ideas for Scrapbooking
Two Ideas published by Barbara Foley
Issue July 2006 - Issue #8046
Issue January 2007- Issue #8052
(I have included them toward the end of this book)

•

134

www.ingramcontent.com/pod-product-compliance
Lightning Source LLC
Chambersburg PA
CBHW021007090426

42738CB00007B/687